for such a time

for such a time

From Transgender to a Son of God

JEFFREY MCCALL

The author has tried to recreate events, locations, and conversations from his memories of them. The author has made every effort to give credit to the source of any images, quotes, or other material contained within and obtain permissions when feasible. Some names and identifying details have been changed or abbreviated to protect the privacy of individuals.

Copyright © 2018 by Jeffrey McCall

All rights reserved. No part of this book may be reproduced or transmitted in any form or by any means, electronic or mechanical, including photocopying, recording, or any information storage and retrieval system, without permission in writing from the author.

ISBN: 978-0-9600463-0-0 - Paperback
eISBN: 978-0-9600463-1-7 - ePub
eISBN: 978-0-9600463-2-4 - mobi

Printed in the United States of America   1 1 2 1 1 8

∞This paper meets the requirements of ANSI/NISO Z39.48-1992 (Permanence of Paper)

Scripture quotations marked "NIV" are taken from the Holy Bible, New International Version®, NIV®. Copyright © 1973, 1978, 1984 by Biblica, Inc.™ Used by permission of Zondervan. All rights reserved worldwide.

First and foremost, I dedicate this book to God the Father, God the son Jesus, and God the Holy Spirit. God has been very kind and loving toward me. The Father has shown me a father's love I didn't know existed. Jesus has shown me a sacrificial love that there are no words for. And the Holy Spirit has shown me a patience I only imagined anyone would have for me. God's love for me has been so unrelenting and faithful to keep me hidden in him.

I also dedicate this book to my parents, Jeff McCall and Gracie Arroyo. To my parents: you are who God chose for me to come through, and I honor you. Thank you, Mom and Dad, for teaching me early about God.

To my brothers, Josh, Caleb, Papo, Carlos, Brian, and Jacob, I love y'all!

To Melissa and Bailey, love y'all so much sisters!

I also dedicate this book to Leah McCall, who has been a great staple in my life.

To both my grandmothers, I love you very much!

To my "Queenie" Esther and Janessa, I love y'all so much! You both are two of the strongest people I know!

To Pastor Jentezen Franklin, thank you for preaching the word of God. The Holy Spirit was using you to sow into my life in my darkest days as Scarlet.

To Janie Weaver Helton . . . what can I say! You have been my best friend through it all! Through God we are now closer than ever. We are brother and sister!

To Kasondra Watkins, thank you so much for being my friend and showing me the ropes!

To Patti Herrington, thank you so much for everything!

To Dr. Sherry Story, you were vital to my story, and I love you and honor your work to help so many students!

I dedicate this book also to Travis Dusseau. Travis always treats me as a brother in Christ and actually took the time to *help love me, disciple me, and show me what a true Christian brother relationship looks like. Nobody has sacrificed more time to help me walk this journey out than him. There is no one else in the world I can be more honest with. I love our long conversations talking about the supernatural power of God!*

To Deborah Griffith Gilchrease, publishing this book would not have been possible without you. You are the reason this book was able to stay in the publishing process. God bless your heart and your obedience to God!

I also dedicate this book to all who have ever been deceived by Satan. There is grace and truth to discover through Jesus Christ. The Holy Spirit is about to release freedom in your life.

By faith Moses, when he had grown up, refused to be known as the son of Pharaoh's daughter. He chose to be mistreated along with the people of God rather than to enjoy the fleeting pleasures of sin.
—Hebrews 11:24–25 (NIV)

Contents

Acknowledgments	xi
Introduction	xiii
Chapter 1: Early Years and the Dream	1
Chapter 2: Teenage Years and Meeting X	9
Chapter 3: Clubs, Parties, and Meeting Y	27
Chapter 4: Nashville, Steve McNair's Death, and Meeting Z	35
Chapter 5: Emmanuel College and Questions	51
Chapter 6: Scarlet, Grad School, and the Psych Ward	57
Chapter 7: Creation, Prophets, and Facebook Live	77
Chapter 8: The Supernatural	85

Acknowledgments

To Kyle Garret, thanks for helping in the editing process! Also a thank-you to Catherine Carlile, Amber Dielman, Jonessa Janet Whiting, Alisha Rochus Heavrin, Kasondra Watkins, Patti Ann Herrington, Dr. June Knight, Pastor Lampley and Mrs. Wanda, Cody Antrim, Ryan McCory, MJ Nixon, Edward Byrd, Kim Zember, Luis Ruiz, Angel Colon, Ronald and Fetima McCray, Joshua Buchanan, Ieacha Lusk, Kayla Brown, Davon Johnson, Darrion Skinner, Kayla Brown, Brooklynn Wojo, Montrea, Ken Williams, Elizabeth Wonning, Gabriel Pagan, David Rivera, and Andrew Jay Medina—you all know your great support!

To Omar Garcia, Bryce Chizek, Evelyn Weber, Jacqueline Kisciras, and Carlos Araiza, thank you for being amazing brothers in Christ! Thank you, Jerry Towns, for all the prayers and talks. You are amazing, brother! And to all my cousins, aunts and uncles, and nieces and nephews, I love you very much!

Introduction

This book is a graphic memoir of my entire life, from my first homosexual thoughts and encounters to supernatural encounters with God. I write about my memories as a young boy and how they affected my perceived sexuality. I also write about years in the club and drug scene, as well as my years in the academic world. I write about being diagnosed with gender dysphoria and how I began living as "Scarlet." All of these things climax into a supernatural encounter with God. This memoir also contains my experiences with God after I became a Christian.

CHAPTER ONE

Early Years and the Dream

I was around six years old when I had the dream. I was sitting in a gymnasium with a wall behind me, looking across the gym toward a door on my right and in front of me. The door opened and two older men came walking through. They wore ancient clothing and had long, white beards and hair. At the time, I didn't know who they were. Later I would get revelation that they were Moses and Elijah. They were talking and taking little notice of me. They walked through the doors on my right and to the opposite end of the building, then exited through the doors on my left. I was left alone in the gym. Suddenly the roof was ripped off by a gigantic bear. The brown bear roared at me furiously. I was terrified and woke up.

The beginning of my life started with memories of my parents. My father is Jeffrey Glenn McCall, and my mother is Gracie Arroyo. When I was born, my maternal grandmother held me and said my hands were blessed. My Mima said I came with the "bread in my hands." As you read my story, you will see I did not think much of this prophecy and never felt like my hands were very blessed.

My parents tried to instill into me at a young age that God was real. I always went to church with my family, including my five brothers, one stepbrother, and two sisters. My brother Caleb and I are the only offspring from my parents' marriage. My grandmothers and I were both close, but my paternal grandmother and I had a particularly close bond. I grew up a lot in her home. My first memory is being left at my paternal grandfather's home with him and his wife, Leonna. I was screaming and crying and could see my parents' backs. I am sure this is a somewhat unideal first memory, but it is mine. I wonder now if many people can recall their first memory; I don't hear people talk about it much. As I grew up, my memories became more vivid and intricate. To follow those maturing memories, we must address an issue that would help the devil shape my life and give me a false identity.

My first memory of any sexual wrongdoing was around age three. I remember an adult male pulling on my underclothing and watching me dance. It was disgusting, and even at that age I knew something was wrong. As the years passed, I was shown parts of his body, and on one occasion I remember he lay on me. I wasn't sure what he was doing. This made me look at men differently at a very young age. I was curious to know what was going on. This is what is so dangerous about molestation: the adult doing the sexually immoral acts doesn't understand the significance of robbing the child's innocence. The individual is being used by Satan as a vessel for the child to be tormented and to start thinking about issues they shouldn't even be pondering until their teenage years. If you have committed these acts, just ask for forgiveness from Jesus and turn from that sin! Jesus has great mercy for all.

We should also be careful what we let youth see as

children. I remember being little and being babysat by a sibling who was watching a film where two women kissed in one scene. I asked my family member why they did that, and she responded she didn't know why they showed that and that "it was stupid." Now, my family member did not do this on purpose, but it is dangerous to let children see this. We have to remember that Jesus talks about misleading children. Satan has to figure out lies to tell every single human being. He starts off young, and he likes to build off those lies. Satan watches and waits for a door of sin to be opened. This is why the Bible says that sin waits at the door! This instance was the beginning of a lie from him to make me think I was attracted to men. Even while writing this, the Holy Spirit has shown me this and is revealing it even more. The situation with the older adult male was the foundation for the future of me thinking I was homosexual and later transgendered. I remember, after these things happened to me, I was more interested in seeing nude men. This was the beginning of an evil that would try to take root in my life.

My parents got divorced when I was around age five. This, of course, was pivotal to my life and my brother's. My parents separated, and Caleb and I lived with my mother and three older brothers: Josh, Papo, and Carlos. The separation especially hurt Caleb; it was the source of much anger in him for years to come. He is a born-again Christian now and has conquered pain through Christ Jesus. In fact, without his help I wouldn't even be writing this book. The separation of my parents hurt me, but it didn't affect me quite the same way. I felt at the time like I evolved with it, but recently God has shown me I just swept this situation under a rug. It bothered me very much, and even after becoming a Christian, he helped me with this deep hurt I didn't even know was there. Caleb and I seemed to love the Lord, as we were young and didn't have sin lording over our lives. During this time, I sometimes wore sheets and pretended they were dresses. I would play with Barbies and other girls' toys. The identity shift the enemy was presenting was beginning to work; after all, living in a fallen world, we are born into sin.

The transition to my teenage years was sudden. The devil knew exactly one of my weak points—love. I was always a romantic. From around age seven or eight, I was reading romance and watching romantic comedies and dramas. I remember being around ten or eleven and reading *Gone with the Wind* for the first time. My mother yelled when she opened the door and saw the hall light on late at night in front of my bedroom: "Are you still up?"

"Yes," I replied, "sorry," and shut the book hastily and turned over.

A kid getting in trouble for reading—that was me. I always loved a happy ending, and I always loved romance. Little did I know then that the greatest love story ever of Jesus and humanity would be revealed to me!

My first attraction or romantic fantasy about a man came around the age of twelve. This is sometimes considered the age of reason; around that age, people can consciously accept Christ and understand what they are doing. I don't think this is a coincidence. The boy I first noticed rode my school bus. I remember feeling attracted to him, but I kept it a secret.

It was the 1990s and homosexuality was now talked about openly, especially in the church. The AIDS pandemic had just begun, and homosexuals were affected in high numbers. Homosexuality was preached against, or at least mentioned, almost every Sunday that I could remember.

Sometimes Christians like to identify others' problems while ignoring their own struggles. Homosexuality is something some Christians like to call out and home in on because many don't have to battle it and therefore feel superior for discussing it. Jesus even says, "Assuredly, I say to you, it will be more tolerable for the land of Sodom and Gomorrah in the day of judgment than for that city!" (Matthew 10:15, NIV). The Lord is saying it will be more tolerable on the day of judgment for Sodom and Gomorrah than the people Jesus Christ preached to and performed miracles for who still wouldn't accept the gospel. So that shows us rejecting the gospel and unbelief actually have a higher cost than what was going in Sodom and Gomorrah!

In middle school, more lies were coming to me from my peers. When a person is told something over and over, they start to believe it. "The tongue has the power of life and death, and those who love it will eat its fruit" (Proverbs 18:21, NIV). People started telling me I was gay and that I acted gay. I was young and didn't even fully understand this, and in the sixth grade I was told this repeatedly. This was also when I started to think of the boy on my school bus in a sexual way. After over a year of hearing it, I gave in and believed it. This is how one lie turns into more. My middle school years were by far the most difficult! I was tortured every day about being different. I was called "queer" and "faggot." I had given in to my thoughts and acted on them, and I started believing what my peers told me. I continued to say I wasn't homosexual, even though in my head I thought I was. Satan had implanted the lie that because other people said it was a real thing, maybe I was gay.

Let's be clear right here, right now: nobody is gay.

That's a lie the enemy uses to destroy someone's life and take away God's plan for somebody. The enemy will do anything to destroy. The Bible says he comes to steal, kill, and destroy. Now, some people are more prone to the lie of homosexuality than others. The devil sees different people's weaknesses when they are young. He plays on that. For example, there is the stereotype of girls with "daddy issues." Their dads weren't there for them, and they crave attention from men. The devil will then at a young age help push them toward being provocative, showing skin, and being more flirtatious with boys to win and maintain those boys' attention. Eventually this can lead to sexual promiscuity, pregnancies, abortions, and so on. So we can see how the chain of sin works to kill, steal, and destroy! This is just one example of how he is going to use the easiest sin that will lure you in as a way to destroy your life. The devil and his demons are not going to work any harder than they have to. Why would they? They have been destroying people's lives for a long time! Satan knows his job well by now. So, he knew little things about me, the past molestation, the softer voice and attitude, the kids telling me I was gay, and he used all these things together to build his lie.

I loved basketball during this time too. I was actually rather good at it. It was a place of escape from my life and problems. I would play all the time at home and at gyms with my father. It was seventh grade, and I was changing both emotionally and physically as a teenager. Of course, my hormones were raging, and I remember several times crying for no reason. I was an emotional wreck half the time. I made the junior high team, but I played one game and quit. I shot one three-pointer and drilled it, and still, the next day, I quit. The boys on the team that year never associated with me or became my friends. I didn't feel part of the team, so I quit.

I feel Satan robbed me of that because if I had continued basketball, I probably would not have joined the friends I did in high school, which was the beginning of drinking and drugs. Satan knew the stability and discipline of basketball was not going to sit well with his plans of destruction, so he let feelings of rejection power that decision. If we look back at forks in our lives, we can see how Satan uses emotions to get us to do what he wants at that time. God would eventually use all of this for his glory.

CHAPTER TWO

TEENAGE YEARS AND MEETING X

My teenage years were the beginning of sin for me. I remember easily transitioning into thinking what people said was true and that I was gay. End of story. I migrated to friendships with girls during this time because, to be honest, they were the only ones who were nice to me. I began some close friendships with them. I started to relate to them. Understandably, when I heard about relationships from the perspectives of girls who were dating males, I started to put myself in those positions. I would think of being with guys and start telling my love stories. This would begin with some close friends of mine.

It was the tenth grade, and I was ready to come out. When I did, my close girlfriends defended me. I simply didn't care anymore. I wasn't going to deny it. I wanted to enter the world of dating and live the way I wanted. The media helped with this. It was the time of the comedy powerhouses *Will & Grace* and *Friends*. Both shows openly promoted homosexual relationships, while *Will & Grace* promoted the female-and-male dynamic of the gay best friend. I watched *Will & Grace* every time it was on and my mother wasn't around. I loved it because there were people like me. They seemed to live these successful lives in wonderful, accepting cities. I could laugh at what they were talking about and feel warm and accepted. *Will & Grace* was making being gay more popular. It was acceptable now for girls to have gay best friends. Hollywood had already been the catalyst for the "gay best friend" idea. Movies such as *Clueless*, *Drive Me Crazy*, *Sweet Home Alabama*, *My Best Friend's Wedding*, *Reality Bites*, and *Mean Girls* all displayed this dynamic. From the 1990s forward, Hollywood and cable pushed this agenda. They helped mold the minds of Millennials to accept homosexuality as normal. That is why in current times Bruce Jenner's transition into trying to become a woman was so popular. This age range that is pushing for support of the LGBTQ community has all been brainwashed by media, writers, and other networks to believe this lie. I believed this lie also, but grace from the Lord Jesus Christ helped me to overcome it and move forward. The media's power is in full force, and giving some examples, I hope, helps show how your mind can be targeted by the enemy.

I was out and openly gay. I didn't care, and years later I was praised by some other homosexual men who told me they wondered how I could come out in high school and not care. I was one of the first in my peer group to do so. Others had longed to, but for some reason I was one of the first to say I was openly gay and not care. The Lord knew my personality, he gave it to me, and later he would use this "all or nothing" personality I have for his kingdom. This was something the Lord saw in me and would use later to let me be a vessel for him. The Lord God of Heaven and Earth saw that when I believed in something enough,

I was not afraid to tell people and live it openly. It's amazing what the Lord can do. He can turn any one of our characteristics into something to use for the kingdom. Even now I think the Lord knew this about us and created us with different gifts that he knows will help bring people into the kingdom. The devil, however, tricked me into using my gift to his advantage.

My female friends and I got into typical teenage trouble. We started to rebel and do whatever we wanted. We were quite bad. We started stealing gas and even clothes from malls. We all began to date boys and have sexual encounters of all types with them. Having cars gave us the freedom to do whatever we wanted, and we did.

I still remember the nervousness of knowing you are about to have sex for the first time. In my sophomore year of high school, I had a female friend who had other gay friends. They were older and were friends of her mother. The guy I was with, whom I shall call B, was a friend of my girlfriend's. He got my number, and it went from there. I met him at a shopping center near my mother's home one day. He was with his gay friend, and the two of them stared me up and down like I was fresh meat. I think the one I wound up having sex with was in his mid to late twenties, and the other man was in his early thirties. B proceeded to say how attractive I was and that he wanted me. With my low self-esteem, I bought it immediately. Here was a guy showing me attention. This is what I had been desperate for. B called more often and acted like he liked me. Little did I know he just wanted to use my body. I made the decision to meet him on a Sunday afternoon. I met up with him and got in the car to go to his house. I was exactly where Satan wanted me. I was about to lose a major portion of my innocence.

Once in the car, B made small talk and decided we should go out in the country to his home in Flat Creek, Tennessee. (Recently I got to drive through that small town on my way to speak for ministry. The Holy Spirit had me get out of the car so I could claim back everything that was taken from me in that place!) B had a beautiful two-story log cabin. I entered his home with him. Immediately he put on some Madonna music, and we started to talk. He poured me alcohol, of course, and we chatted, not long at all. I would estimate we talked less than half an hour, and then we were upstairs and in his bedroom. It all began, and I had my first experience with homosexual intercourse. I remember lying there embarrassed after it was all over and feeling ready to go home.

As he drove me home, I don't even remember any conversation. He dropped me off at the shopping center nearby and I walked to my house. No one was home. I started some laundry for the school week and stood there hearing the roaring water fill the washing machine. I felt changed. I had gone from being a young boy to feeling older in just a couple of hours. I felt I had grown up, but I didn't feel it was in a good way. My innocence had been robbed from me, and I really could feel it. In the coming weeks, I learned about homosexual sex. I thought sex meant you would fall in love with someone and always be with them, but I never heard from B or saw him again until six years later when I was around twenty-one. I saw him at the country club where he worked. He waited on me and my friend L, who had taken me there. I told L he was the one I had first had sex with. She asked me if I was going to talk to him. When he came back I said, "Hey, I'm Jeffrey . . . I haven't seen you in years."

He replied with something like, "Hey, how you been?

Let me know if y'all need anything else." The cold reply let me know what I meant to him.

Exactly one week after my first sexual experience came the tragedy of my brother Joshua. He was the oldest of my brothers on my mother's side. Joshua had a rough life growing up. My mother was young when she had become pregnant with him, only sixteen, and she had given him up because of her lifestyle. She was doing cocaine and hanging out with Colombian and Cuban drug dealers in the infamous late-1970s Miami. The city was known for its rough streets, and my mother was running in them. She was hanging out with drug dealers when the home she was in was robbed. Some hitmen were told to kill her because the drug dealers she was hanging out with thought it was she who had helped with the robbery. She was eventually shot in a bar and taken to a hospital.

Now I know the spiritual context of this shooting. My mother would eventually go on to interpret for different ministers and help share gospel. Satan didn't want her to fulfill this destiny. He also knew she would birth me and my brother Caleb. We both share the gospel of Jesus Christ, and he didn't want that to happen. When something like this happens, look and you can find the spiritual actions behind major, life-threatening situations. After the shooting, her mother, the one who would eventually prophesy over me at my birth, was there for her and told her she had to accept and live for Jesus. Around this time, Joshua and my brother Carlos were in foster care. They were removed and cared for by my grandmother and Aunt Carol. After my mother gave her life to Jesus, she moved to Huntsville, Alabama, and was in a wonderful Christian ministry called Teen Challenge—later my brother Caleb would go to a men's branch of the same ministry for help with his drug and alcohol problems. There my mother sobered up and got Joshua and Carlos back. Joshua loved my mother no matter what. He got to be back with her, and I am sure as a child he was so happy.

Just as we all have things we struggle with, my brother Joshua struggled with drugs and alcohol. He started having seizures sometime in his early twenties. I don't know for sure, but it has been speculated that some of the harsh drugs such as ecstasy and acid could have been the cause. He never had seizures until he was a young adult. One seizure was so bad it put him in ICU in a Huntsville hospital. I remember visiting him with my mother when I was young. He was so sick. He pulled through and moved out of Huntsville to Shelbyville, Tennessee, where my mother and I were living. He lived less than a mile from my house. He would always verbalize that he didn't want me to live a homosexual lifestyle. Right before his death, it had caused some division between us. I decided to avoid him when I could. I do remember an afternoon where he and I got to hang out alone. He suggested we watch a movie, and I asked him if he would watch *Legally Blonde*. I liked the film and thought the story was funny, seeing as I had always wanted to be a lawyer and help people. He watched it with me and we laughed. Although I have lots of memories with Joshua because we grew up together, this memory is one of my favorites.

The week between my sexual encounter and Joshua's tragedy was his birthday. Even though we were not really talking, I called him. I still remember the old yellow phone I called him on. It was plugged into the wall beside my bed in the upstairs loft of my mother's home. I called and said happy birthday, and we talked for maybe thirty seconds. That Sunday I was with my friend Leslie out at her farm.

The next week was our spring break, so I would be going to Florida with my dad for the Cincinnati Reds spring training. (My dad was a scout for them.) I was sitting with her and the call came to my cell phone. It was my mom. I figured she was going to wish me a good week in Florida, but she was screaming and crying. I couldn't understand at first. Then she said, "He is dead. Joshua is dead." She screamed and screamed it over and over.

I found out where she was and said, "I am on my way."

Leslie was also upset as she drove me there. She had been in a sexual relationship with Joshua for some time. I still remember pulling in the driveway to where he lived. I remember the ambulance lights, the police, and my mom on the ground crying. She was hysterical. It hadn't really kicked in for me yet. I watched them take him out of the house with a white covering. He was dead. My brother was dead. My oldest brother, the person I felt most protected with, was gone. I never felt more protected in all my life than when I was with him.

Death is so final. There is no "I am sorry" left to say on this earth. There are no more conversations. There isn't a hug or a kiss. It is a final feeling that you can only understand once you fully experience it with someone close. It's almost as if the world stops spinning for a second. It's quiet even if it's hectic around. You know something deep, something surreal, has happened. It's even hard to explain now, but I can feel it.

The whole way to the hospital, all I could think was *Lord, please don't take him.* I would say in my head, *I don't really know he is dead; I haven't seen his face.* I knew I would have to see him before I could believe it. I remember thinking, *If he lives, Lord, I'll come to the hospital every day. I'll read him his favorite books, and I will sit by his bed until he* comes to God. I can deal with him being in ICU, but I can't deal with him being dead.

The relationship between us was never mended. He was gone from this earth, and I found out for sure when I got to hospital. I was told he was dead, and the close family were all allowed to see his body in a private little room once we felt we could go in. I went in alone. It was horrible. The white covering was pulled back, and I could see his face and his eyes open. There was no response. I said his name, and there was still no response. I haven't cried and let some grief out over this in a long time until now. But it is real, and death is real. I remember crying and leaving the room. I went and sat in the room they have for families who are experiencing a loss. I was devastated and felt more alone. What was I going to do without him?

I later got to ask my mother what had happened. We had gone to a local steakhouse the day he died for Caleb's birthday—he and Joshua had the same birthday. My mother had called to invite Joshua to come eat with us, but he had not answered. He worked two jobs at that time, so we assumed he was at work. I remember feeling relieved he hadn't answered the phone. I was avoiding him because he had made comments about me being homosexual and didn't want me to live like that. I had somewhat accepted it. I was always trying to hide it from my parents, so I didn't want to be around Joshua. The tension between us was obvious, and my mother would ask what was going on. So I felt relieved when he didn't answer and for years carried that guilt.

I remember seeing him a few weeks before he died. I was driving by and looked right at him as he was walking to work, making eye contact, and I didn't even pick him up. That also plagued me for years, but there is no condemnation in Christ. I know Christ forgives me, and I know if my brother were here, he would forgive me also. Sometimes I can still see those eyes looking back at me. You are always forgiven by the Lord when you ask, but some things you have done you will never forget.

My mother had gone to his house to check on him. He didn't answer when she knocked, and she opened the door to find him lying there with his hands outstretched to the phone, which was off the hook. I still hate that he was alone when he died, and probably terrified. That part is so horrible. I wish that for nobody. I think that was one of the worst aspects of his death for me.

Family came in from other states. My home was filled with aunts and uncles and cousins. They all tried to console my mother. Aunt Carol was of course the best at that. Aunt Carol was always one of my favorites of my mom's sisters. I remember going to the funeral home with her and my mother. My mother saw Joshua in the casket before the people arrived for the visitation. The grief hit her so hard that as she cried hysterically, she fell straight down on the ground. It was like watching someone so full of grief they could not stand. Aunt Carol helped her to sit on a bench.

I remember walking up to the casket and seeing Joshua in it. His hair was braided in cornrows, just like he loved it. His eyes were closed now. He felt cold, stiff, and I knew he was empty. He was not there. Family from my mother's side as well as my father's poured in to support the family. Joshua's friends, employees, and others poured in from churches to support my family. I still remember my friend Janie coming to be by my side. She is still to this day one of my best friends. Having her there meant so much to me. I was a pallbearer and helped carry my brother to the hearse that was going to take his body to the grave. I sat beside my cousin Susie from Miami at the funeral. I remember Aunt Barbara crying when they went to lower him into the grave. She ran up to the casket and was stopped by someone. Joshua was lowered into the ground, and the dirt was laid upon the casket. I don't even remember leaving or how I got home. It was cold, I remember that. We got home and were in mourning. My brother was gone, I was angry, and the devil was going to use this anger against me in the form of rebellion.

After the encounters with sex and death all in one week, the alcohol and drugs quickly followed. I remember a cousin of mine and some of the girlfriends I hung out with would drink together. It was a Friday night, and I had lied to my parents about where I was. I was at my cousin's house and her mother, my aunt, was gone. I drank whiskey for the first time. I drank until I was blackout drunk. I remember when I first caught the buzz, I thought, *Wow, this is great.* Some of the anxiety loosened. Little did I know, alcohol would come to haunt my unsaved life more than once. My friends had to put me in the shower because I passed out and was throwing up everywhere. I could hear them but could not see them. It was a horrible experience, but that was my first.

After my brother died, I moved in with my father. My mother was distraught and also trying to keep a marriage together, and since Caleb and I were teenagers now, she thought it best we live with my dad. We moved with my dad and stepmom to another city. We were immediately enrolled in a private Christian school called Highland Rim Academy. At Highland Rim Academy, I immediately was drawn to the two girls in high school who were even somewhat relatable. One girl, Rachel, I had known previously because her mother and my mother were friends.

We had played dolls together when we were young. Rachel suffered from an eating disorder I would later have struggles with: bulimia. She was a kind girl. The other girl, Jamie, was not so kind to me at that time. We are actually now friends. Jamie and Rachel were best friends, and now I entered their group. I told them I felt gay because my other girlfriends in public school had been accepting of it. Jamie didn't like it or agree with it most of the time. She wanted me prayed for. She was trying to help, but she was young and didn't understand fully how to handle it. At this school, I would meet a teacher who was willing to help.

The teacher was a kind lady, the daughter of the preacher who had started the school. She really did want the best for me and would talk to me about her problems growing up. She told me her story of how she was molested when she was young. She would pray for me, and you could tell she knew how upset I was by my big brother Joshua's death. She earnestly did try to help me see the change I could have. I was young, immature, and hurt by the things that had already happened to me. I listened but wasn't seeing much change.

I remember one day at a Wednesday-night group meeting I told Rachel and Jamie I was having inappropriate thoughts about a boy in the youth group. The girls swept me to a back room and prayed for me. Looking back, these girls were trying to help me but didn't know the right way to go about it, and I was clueless on how to surrender to the Lord. It truly is all about surrender. You can always pray for someone to change, and God hears you and can help work out things for that person to have openness to the Lord. But you can pray and scream at someone that they are a sinner all day, and for the most part, you won't help them. It sometimes can even bring them more guilt. I believe the individual has to feel the conviction of sin from the Holy Spirit and then realize Jesus's blood will cover it and wash it away. The sinner has to understand grace: that God has mercy on them through Jesus Christ. It is about letting the Holy Spirit melt that blockage around the heart. I was not ready to surrender my life to Jesus and follow him.

This teacher who helped me and the youth pastor of this church were later caught having an affair. She was struggling with her own issues, but I will never forget her kindness and how she tried to help me. I do not judge her, and if you did reading this, check your heart. We have all fallen short of the glory of God and made mistakes. I appreciate what she did for me and other students. I often wonder where she is today and hope the Lord has healed her from the struggles Satan used against her. "Because judgment without mercy will be shown to anyone who has not been merciful. Mercy triumphs over judgment" (James 2:13, NIV).

I went for a short time to Highland Rim. Later I was taken out and got to go back to my hometown school of Shelbyville Central High. My junior year I had a few friends and wasn't getting into too much trouble. Then came the summer before my senior year. I was desperate to lose weight. I wasn't huge, but I wanted to be rail thin. This was when the eating disorders started. That summer I cut back my eating drastically. Some of the girls I was then hanging out with had mentioned something about throwing up after they had eaten meals. I thought, *Wow I can eat, and then get rid of it.*

Some days that summer I didn't eat at all, or I would just eat a peach or apple for the whole day and then sit in my room after work and watch television. Paris Hilton and Nicole Richie were ruling the airways. *The Simple Life* had come out, and I looked up to these girls. They were everything I wanted to be: thin, rich, and glamorous. Britney Spears had also came out during my middle school years. In high school she was my favorite celebrity. I idolized her: the dancing, the hair extensions, the notoriety, the glamour, the parties, and the boyfriends.

I wanted all of these things, and to begin I had to get thin. I started missing meals, and then, when I would eat, I would throw up everything. At the start of my senior year, I dropped between thirty and forty pounds. I remember coming to school wearing a new black polo to distinguish the effect of my weight loss. Some of my peers were saying, "Wow, Jeffrey, you look great." I felt I had been noticed, and now it was my time to become more of who I thought I wanted to be. They didn't know how I really felt: empty and hungry!

During my senior year I met X, the boy whom I would eventually think was my first love. He played the guitar and was kind of a bad-boy type who did drugs and was somewhat different. He showed me an ounce of attention, and I jumped like a puppy. I still remember the first time he looked at me, just staring at me with his crooked grin. It felt like the beginning of life for me. Someone was really looking at me.

As time progressed, I eased into his life and he into mine. I was spending time with him every day, and I loved it. The drugs of ecstasy and cocaine were rampant in my town. X and I were doing some of these drugs every weekend, and sometimes together throughout the school week. X also happened to be in the same lunch block as me even though he was a grade younger. He sat beside me at lunch, and I loved that the other girls noticed how close we had gotten. Soon the rumors started: Jeffrey and X were hanging out a lot, what was it? I fueled that fire and watched it burn. I was so happy I wouldn't be alone—or so I thought.

The drugs continued, and sometime in my first semester of my senior year, X and I messed around and then later had sexual intercourse. I really fell for him when he showed concern for me. Just to get his full attention, I called him one night after I tried to hurt myself. I swallowed several blood-pressure pills and started to feel dizzy and weak. I had been depressed because I wanted X to love me. He answered his phone and talked me through throwing up the pills. I wanted his attention so bad.

Our relationship started dwindling after his mother caught him trying to get ecstasy for me one night when we were "rolling" on the drug. I threw a fit because my high was coming down and I wanted more drugs. I threw such a fit he called the drug dealer and had him bring us more at around two or three in the morning. X got caught coming back in the door by his mother, and she could tell he was high. I wasn't someone his mother wanted him hanging out with anymore. By Christmas, we weren't hanging out as much, and in the beginning of the spring semester, another boy told people at school what had happened with me and X. Later that spring, a friend of mine decided to date him, and that drilled the nail in that coffin.

X had been hurt in life also. He had been through a hard time himself and had lost his father at an early age. He was hurting as much as I was, but I didn't know that then. His mother had been hurt also. She was a sweet lady, and I pray for them and their family now that all things will work out for them in and through Christ Jesus.

When X didn't want me anymore, I was even more depressed. I went to the doctor sad, depressed, and upset. I had little time to talk, so I told him about some weird experiences I was having. I had episodes where I was panicky and couldn't breathe. One time I had woken up in a state of panic. He prescribed the Satan incarnate of pills: Xanax. This would start my twelve-year cycle of pill abuse. After taking the first one, I felt amazing! I could take them and feel happy and relaxed. This was my heaven—or so I thought.

Around this time Aunt Carol, whom I loved so much, died. I had been very close to Aunt Carol. She was my only maternal aunt who had no children. She had taken care of me and all of my cousins in some way, shape, or form. She was kind and loved us all so much. We were her little babies, even when we grew up. My life wouldn't be the same without her. She left an impact on me I can never forget. She always stuck by her faith and the Bible on me living a homosexual lifestyle. She never made me feel bad or inadequate about it—she plain out told me it wasn't right.

I remember my love for her, though, and her love for me. She asked me to take her to the airport when she was moving from Tennessee to Miami to live with my grandmother. She had MS, and it was getting worse. She wanted to be with my grandmother, and so she moved. She left everything behind, including her affair with a married Indian man that she knew was wrong. She died about a year after the move. "Tata," as we called her, loved sweets and would call things the funniest names. She had always spoken Spanish for the most part, so her English sometimes was so funny. She would tell me to get her some Sprite Zyrtec, which meant Sprite Remix. I can't even remember what she called Sonic birthday-cake shakes, but it was something funny. I remember she ordered a Big N' Nasty at McDonald's once—she meant a Big N' Tasty. Oh, how I miss her.

I went to Miami during the first semester of my senior year to go to her funeral. I remember being so sad she was gone. The night before the visitation, I had that panic attack coming out of my sleep, unable to breathe and feeling so alone and scared. This was the situation that got me into the doctor's office. I once got so messed up on the Xanax when I was at my friend's house and dealing with the separation from X. I called him slurring and cussing him out, and then lay there on the bed totally messed up. I was hurt by him leaving, my brother dying, my aunt dying, and my new sexual identity as a homosexual. I was so lost and hurt. This life was turning out to be unbearable!

Around the middle of my senior year, I was moved into a new group of friends. I felt popular and had a new identity as the gay male in the class. I was friends with all the pretty girls, and the straight guys didn't give me problems; they wanted to date all my friends. I started having some promiscuous sex around this time. There was a phone chatline for homosexual men. I would get on there and meet guys for hookups. I would lie about my age, being under eighteen at this time. I think most guys knew I was underage, but they just wanted sex from me; they didn't care about my age.

My senior year was ending, and I was soon going to graduate. Even though now I have a bachelor's degree and have gone to graduate school, I barely graduated high school due to absences. I had become lazy, and some days didn't even go to school. My life was filled with drinking, pot, ecstasy, and cocaine. I even tried crystal meth for the first time. The drugs had taken over the drinking, and I was constantly trying to be high. I would skip school and go and do cocaine with friends at people's homes. I hung out with drug dealers and even one stripper. It wasn't the crowd I needed to be with, but I didn't care. I was trying to cope, and I thought the drugs were helping. In my mind, the cocaine and uppers just helped maintain my weight. These drugs kept me thin, along with my newfound bulimia.

I don't know how high school is today with eating disorders, but when I was growing up, the girls were all doing something for the most part. It wasn't always talked about, but most of us knew. My father at one point had told me I was overweight after my brother's death. I went into immediate weight-loss mode. After my brother's death when I was fifteen, I was totally empty and tried to fill the emptiness with food, so I had gained some weight. After my dad's comment, I decided it must come off. I lost it with the newfound drugs and eating disorder. I would go to a friend's house every afternoon and eat. We were hungry, like most teenagers after school. I would even tell her I was going to throw up after our food. It was normal for me, and I didn't care who knew. I told all my friends.

One afternoon, my father knocked on my door. I had reached a pretty low weight, and my collarbone and ribs were noticeable. He asked me if I needed a rehab for people with eating disorders. I talked my way out of it and put on a little more weight after this experience. The devil was using my emptiness and low self-esteem to make me think being more skinny and attractive would help me be more desirable to men. It was around this time that I also started to cut myself. I had noticed other friends who had done it, so I started too. I really wasn't a shower cutter. I would cut myself with knives and then always keep them in a place where I could hide them. I felt it released some pain—some form of the screaming individual inside could get out. It was a horrible thing to do, and thank God above none of them ever got infected.

Graduation day was coming. I had missed so many days, around sixty, so the principal called my father. I spent some days after school making up missed time so I could graduate in the spring with my friends. I was still doing drugs and would tell my teachers in the mornings I had to go to the bathroom every period. In the bathroom, I would snort cocaine and come back to class. I was ready to be done with high school. I thought this great, big, mysterious world was out there. I was going to move eventually to a city, have a boyfriend, and get an apartment. I was looking forward to transitioning to my new life and becoming independent from rules and regulations.

CHAPTER THREE

CLUBS, PARTIES, AND MEETING Y

I remember turning eighteen on May 5, 2005. My first gay club experience was on this date. I went to the gay club called Play. It was in Nashville, and it was the new happening nightclub. I went with girlfriends, a heterosexual male friend, and my cousin. My cousin was a drag queen, and we had to go to his house first to meet up with him. He was going to ride with us. We got in the car and went to the club. Once there, we all were on something, though I don't quite remember what we were doing that night. I think it was ecstasy. I remember so many men there looking at me. I felt wanted. I felt attractive. I was young and fresh to them, something new. I remember being floored that there were no barriers between the urinals. Men were all looking at each other's private areas. It was my first experience being in public with all these homosexual men. During the drag show, I got a call on my cell phone. My friend was screaming that they were at the car. One girlfriend screamed that the other girl was dead. I still remember this because I ran to the car. I was thinking, *Oh my gosh. I have dealt with death so much already.* My parents had always made me scared of the city anyway. I ran to find my friends standing beside the car we had come in. They were laughing. She wasn't dead. It was a joke. They didn't realize I had dealt with so much death before. I had panicked, thinking it was real. I will never forget that night.

The summer after my eighteenth birthday, I moved into an apartment with my friend Chasity. We moved to the square in the old, unique Gunter Building. It was this amazing old building from around the 1920s with apartments on the third and fourth floors. The apartment was the scene of many late-night parties and drug escapades. I was drinking and going out almost every night on a slew of miscellaneous drugs. I was working and going to college at this time also. I dropped out the first semester of my freshmen year. I was tired and constantly juggling working, school, and drugs.

Once I dropped out of college, doing drugs became even more a part of my life. I overdosed and had to go to the hospital in October. I had been with my cousin and a friend partying for days. I had brought ecstasy pills. I will never forget they were red and, I think, double or triple stack. (That means the size of the actual pill.) I took them and gave my cousin and friend some. We took them for three days. We went to an after-hours club and partied with all our friends. We were so high on crystal meth and ecstasy that I felt like the music playing out of the speakers was flowing out of me. I was so high I didn't eat for three days. By the end of the binge, I had one pill left. I remember taking it on an empty stomach, which was so empty I felt where the pill landed. I was immediately in high gear. This ecstasy pill was like no other. I had been up so long that when it hit me, it exploded my senses!

My vision turned upside down and I ran outside. My

cousin just stood at the door yelling at me to get inside and that I was going to get them in trouble if I went to the hospital. Drugs make people particularly selfish. My friend J came over and helped me out. He talked me down through the anxiety and eventually brought me inside and calmed me down. He let me lie in his bed while he went in the room with my cousin to do more drugs. I lay in the bed thinking and not really sleeping. Before I had gone to bed, my friend J's boyfriend had told me to come in his room. He made me feel uncomfortable and asked if I wanted to watch porn! Really, watch porn, when I had just tripped out and almost died.

The next day, a friend came to pick me up. She drove my car and me home to Shelbyville. I was still so high I had a panic attack and had to have her pull over. When I got home, I was messed up for days and eventually went to the hospital again. I went to the hospital twice in the next couple of days. I couldn't sleep well, so the doctors gave me a pill that knocked me out that night. When I woke up in a panic, I knew something wasn't right. My father eventually came to visit me. He told me I was too skinny. He took me home with him to another city. I stayed with him for a couple of days, but then made him think I was okay to go home. I went home, and I remember lying on my friend Chasity's bed and watching TBN for days. My friend Chasity would come in and see what I was watching and ask about it. She could see I had turned and glanced at God. But that wouldn't last long.

Around spring of the next year, when I was nineteen years old, I met a man whom I will call Y. My cousin had known Y for many years. They were party buddies. I didn't even realize until months into the relationship that I had seen him before, and not just in pictures. My cousin had kept those pictures in a box when I was a teenager. I would think to myself, *That is the type of guy I want to be with when I move into the gay scene.* I had also seen Y working as a bartender at a restaurant in Manchester, Tennessee, when I was fifteen, the week my brother died. My aunt and cousin had been trying to console me. For some reason, they had taken me to a restaurant for drinks. I looked old enough, I guess, and it worked. While having a margarita, I noticed the bartender. My female cousin noticed him too and said he was attractive and probably gay. I noticed him and he was very attractive, but I didn't realize it was Y, my cousin's friend. I had only seen him in pictures at that point. Years later, I would tell Y I had seen him when I was fifteen. I finally met Y in person at a club around early 2006. He was nice enough but didn't show any real interest in me. Soon, though, I had an email from him on my Myspace account. He was interested and officially asked me out for dinner. I was so excited. This is what I had always wanted—or so I thought.

 The Y years were from around age nineteen to twenty-two. Our first date didn't go as planned. He had been high on crystal meth and didn't have great timing due to the drugs. He showed up at my friend's house, where I was staying with her and her boyfriend. When I saw the BMW pull up, I was in awe. I thought, *Here is a tall, good-looking man with money, a career as a realtor, and a name in the gay scene.* When he arrived, he was tired and wanted to lie in the bed. I had learned to not have sex quickly if you truly liked the guy. He just spit a lot of game and eventually went to bed. He told me how good looking I was and that he wanted to marry and be with someone like me. I bought it hook, line, and sinker! It was the bait that I took, and he knew how to reel me in!

Once I eventually gave in and had sex with him, it was the beginning of emotional and spiritual attachment to him. That is what is so lethal about sexual sin. It ties you in with the person and connects you in ways you do not need to be connected. The devil uses it to hurt people and have their focus on sex and not God. Sex is special and holy when consecrated in marriage between a man and woman. Homosexual relationships a lot of the time try to mimic heterosexual ones. In most homosexual relationships, there is a more masculine individual and a more feminine individual. Anyone can see this in both male and female homosexual relationships. It's almost a natural drawing deep inside of the people involved to have a relationship like God intended.

For years, my life was consumed with my love for Y. I remember Y first bringing me to his parents' home. His father had a large house out in the country. Y brought me there to meet his family. I could tell he did get some looks from family members because he was in his early thirties and I was only nineteen. What I came to find out was that Y was not as glamorous as I had thought. His name was somewhat popular in the scene because he was a known drug dealer. He was also homeless, and though he was working as a realtor, a vast majority of his money was going to drugs, crystal meth in particular. He would "sketch out" after staying up for days.

I would go outside to smoke a cigarette when we would be at his realty office. One time I came back and the door was locked. When I knocked, he opened the door with a hammer in his hand. He was paranoid from the drugs. He thought the people across the road getting gasoline at the gas station were coming for him. I felt bad for him because I could tell he really thought someone was conspiring against him. I had never seen anyone act like this. I remained sober for the majority of the time I dated Y. What I had seen, I didn't want to become. Also, the overdosing from the year before had scared me. I'll never forget asking the doctor in the ER if I was going to die. She had replied, "Most of the time when people ask that, it's not good!" I think she went about this the wrong way, but it was enough to scare me.

Y was using a majority of the time. He was usually high and would work in a manic stage and then sleep for days. I didn't keep a job this whole time, and my whole attention was on keeping Y happy. I was constantly trying to find him or, when I was with him, trying to constantly please him. One time when I was with him, we were arguing and things were getting heated. He jerked me around a little and then came to hit me, but my friend, who owned the home we lived in, interceded.

My life with Y was miserable, and I had to do anything sexually he asked for. Sometimes the sex hurt, but he would talk me into continuing what he wanted. I remember him buying sex toys and telling me he was going to use them with me. I thought this was exciting, but when they were used, I just felt like a dirty thing he used to derive his pleasure from. He constantly was going out with other men and younger guys, and I felt like I couldn't keep up with him. My already-low self-esteem was going even lower. I felt bad about myself most of the time. He also would verbally abuse me. He was quite a bit older, and when I didn't understand something he would say, I was stupid. He was a good manipulator, too. He could talk me into most anything; I always believed his lies. I felt he was my future husband, and I loved him so much. I was young, and that feeling of wanting to please a man and have him love me was so strong. These years were very hard.

At one point when Y and I were taking one of our many breaks, he was arrested for drugs. He was busted with crystal meth and ecstasy tablets—a serious charge. He was incarcerated, and his family paid the 10 percent of the $130,000 bond to get him out. On getting out, he called me.

One day, when we were in Nashville dealing with something he had to do regarding his arrest, I got a call that I was accepted into some government housing I had applied for. When I agreed to the contract, we moved into an apartment in Shelbyville, Tennessee. I thought it was perfect timing—we would have our own apartment. I tried to make it as homey as I could. I worked at a gas station as a cashier, and Y worked at a restaurant in the neighboring city. Y would disappear for days, and then at times he would be home. I would try to clean, cook, and keep things nice for us, but I was also partying. I started drinking a lot and even doing crystal meth occasionally. I remember one night partying with some girlfriends. An African American girl who was in the neighbor's apartment was getting beat up by a man. We could hear the screams through the wall. My friends and I called the police, and they came. The girl was left out on the street with her baby and the man taken to jail. I remember seeing Christ's love that night when one of the girls, Sara, helped the girl out. She took her to get food and drinks, then she took her to a hotel and paid for her room for the night. She left the party to do all this. See, that is the thing about Christ's love—it comes in all shapes and forms when people are willing to do it. When she returned, we asked her about it, and she said Jesus would have wanted her to do it and had compelled her to do it. I love her still and am friends with her to this day.

Living in this home with Y had taken a toll on me. It had showed me once again he didn't love me. I remember getting sick and having an infected hair. It grew into an infected cyst, and doctors had to break it open. The pain was severe, so the doctors prescribed me pain pills. Pain pills were something I didn't ever abuse. I just didn't like the way they made me feel. I told Y what had happened, and I couldn't work for days. I sat alone at my apartment. Y was gone during this time on a drug escapade. My Aunt Kathy helped me and brought me food and checked on me. Because of the location of the abscess, it was hard to walk, and I had to lie down for several days to let it heal. I was depressed, sick, and alone.

Around this time, I visited the after-hours club called Kiss. This eventually would change owners and later be called Club 508. There is where I started snorting crystal meth again. I would get drunk and then snort the crystal meth and stay up for a day or two. During this time, I started thinking about my relationship with Y and what I felt about him. I told him I was moving out of our apartment in Shelbyville and would be moving in with friends in Nashville. This occurred when I was around twenty-two years old. I thought this would be a fresh new start. I would leave Y and my hometown of Shelbyville behind for good.

CHAPTER FOUR

Nashville, Steve McNair's Death, and Meeting Z

I moved in with two friends of mine, a gay couple. They lived near Hermitage outside Nashville. I got a job at the local Cracker Barrel, and my drinking continued heavily. I met a girl all of us at work called Jenny. I remember the day I met her. She was a beautiful Persian girl, and all the other girls at work didn't like her. They were jealous of her beauty, and I knew it. I was always drawn to girls whom the other girls didn't like, and we were instantly friends. She made a lot of money and was a hard worker, often picking up shifts other servers didn't want. I remember we exchanged phone numbers and hung out often. We would drink together and started partying together. Jenny was having an affair with a guy at work. Both this guy and Jenny had other people they were dating, and Jenny was living with a man at this time.

I remember breaking into apartment community pools at late hours or early morning. We were drinking and wanting to have fun. Jenny had low self-esteem like I did and would give in to sexual advances from other guys. I remember her and this guy from work having sex right in front of me in the hot tub. We were all drunk and didn't think a thing about it. This shows just how lax the alcohol made us all. Now it seems crazy to think about the stuff I saw, did, and was part of in the world! I remember another night getting so drunk I could barely walk and going to a strip club with Jenny and this male from work. I was so drunk I fell onto a table beside us and needed help getting up. After this, we went to the gay club and partied more there. Then we went to a second strip club.

This was my life: drinking and partying nonstop. During this time, I explored even more sexual promiscuity. Before, I had at least been trying to be with just one person. Jenny and I both were promiscuous. We would talk about our lives and how we wanted to live one day. We both wanted rich older men who would take care of us.

Our religious backgrounds were quite different. Jenny was part of the religion Zoroastrianism. She didn't know Christ, and I wish I would have known how to share Christ with her. I only mentioned I believed in Jesus somewhat, but I wasn't showing her the truth of Christ because I didn't know him myself. I didn't have the Holy Spirit guiding my steps daily; I was doing what I wanted to every day.

One of the last times I hung out with Jenny, we got dressed nice and went to the mall at Green Hills in Nashville. I had gone there since I was young and told her it was where the people with money went. I told her we could possibly meet older, wealthy men. We walked around the mall; afterward, we went to look at Cadillac Escalades. Jenny wanted one bad. We looked at several that day near Green Hills and in other areas. She couldn't get approved for one because they were so expensive. She told me eventually a rich man would buy one for her.

A couple of years later, I was lying out in the backyard of an older couple I worked for as their caregiver. They would take a daily afternoon nap, and when they did, I would lie out and tan. As I lay out, I was listening to the radio. I heard the football quarterback for the Tennessee Titans in Nashville had been murdered. They said it was a murder-suicide. I thought it was sad but didn't think much more about it. My aunt on my father's side, whom I was close to and spoke regularly with, called and asked me if I had seen the front of the Tennessean newspaper. She told me the girl who had killed Steve McNair looked like one of the friends I had described to her. The older couple I took care of got the newspaper regularly, so I decided to read the article the next day. Sure enough, there it was on the front page: a picture of Jenny. The name printed was her real name, Sahel Kazemi, her Persian name that she never went by in America.

I was in shock. Jenny had killed the quarterback and had also killed herself. It was so heartbreaking and so real because it was so final. I had just thought about Jenny the week earlier. I was planning on calling her one day, but I didn't have a charger to the old phone that had her number in it. I thought, *Is this real life?* It seemed so surreal. Later, on a television special, I saw the last video Jenny was ever in. She was getting arrested for DUI. McNair was with her. He didn't get arrested and went home. The story was she got out and went to an apartment McNair was paying for. There she met up with him and shot him on the couch and then shot herself in the head after she lay down beside him. The police found out she had purchased a gun from a convicted murderer.

When I watched the video the police released of her being arrested the night before, I noticed something. She was driving a black Cadillac Escalade. She had gotten what she wanted: an older man with money and her Cadillac Escalade. She had to pay with her life. The life she dreamed of having was nothing but misery. He was probably going to leave her since he had a wife. This is not known for sure to be the reason she was upset, but that is my guess. She was also doing drugs and drinking during this time with him. I remember her drinking very little when we hung out and never doing drugs at all. I assume she started drug use during this time. I still to this day think about her and how I should have showed her Christ. I was lost at this time also and didn't do what I needed to do. Sin looks glamorous, but it really isn't. She was my first friend who would commit suicide, but not the last.

During this time, I was working for a family by the name of Coke in the Nashville area. My drug use increased, and I was big into the after-hours club scene. These clubs would open around 12:00 or 1:00 a.m. and stay open till 8:00 or 9:00 a.m. Then there would be after parties with the owners and personal friends. I became friends with the owner of one such club and got into promoting parties. I moved into an apartment with a lady who was in the scene and also a drug dealer. During this time, I started doing drugs myself and selling petty amounts to keep my habit up. I was so lonely and getting lonelier inside the world of crystal meth.

Crystal meth is known for its powerful stranglehold over people. It attacks your soul. If you have never done it, then it is hard to describe. It makes you so lonely, even being around a crowd of people you could feel depressed all the time. This is the life I had seen Y in and wanted to avoid, and now I was in it. The life of speed I was around was very different from what is typically shown. What is typically shown is people who use homemade bathtub crank. I never did that stuff. I used what we called "tina" or "ice," which was transported from Mexico. The people I was around never had holes in their faces; they brushed their teeth, and they were constantly tanning, doing hair, and wearing makeup. No one in the circles I ran in was overweight, and for the most part everyone looked like a rock star. It was, however, like being around a bunch of soulless people. Everyone was selfish, vindictive, and sleeping around.

It all looked well to me. Sin is always fun for a season, and even the Bible tells us that. I thought I was having so much fun. The promotion I did for the club was going well. My first party was called the White Party. People were supposed to wear white-themed clothing, and I decorated the club in a winter style since it was December. The party was a hit, and that made my name known throughout the after-hours Nashville club scene. I even had a big drug dealer tell me, "Welcome, you are in now." I moved out of the apartment where I lived with a friend and moved into another place. Once again, I was living with some gay friends. Now I was doing crystal meth and bringing guys home all the time.

During this time, I fell for a guy who was a street hustler. He was attractive to me, but he dated girls. I thought of this as a challenge, and I knew the drugs could lure him in. I moved him in with me. He would lie to me all the time and even steal from me, but I loved that all the people in the drug scene I was in were talking about this attractive straight guy living with me in the apartment. Scene people were also talking about my White Party. I had drugs now all the time and was always around the drug dealers. I was high every day. One of these days, I met Z. He lived downtown in the newer area of Nashville called "The Gulch." It was trendy, and I thought, *I like him, and he's nice to me. I will finally have a nice guy to take care of me.* That was one thing I always felt: the need to be taken care of. I always felt so vulnerable. The Lord has shown me this about my personality. Now I trust in my Father, the creator of heaven and earth. Who could take better care of me?

He started seeing me, and finally we decided I would move in with him in February of 2010 when the lease was up at the apartment I was in. Z made me happy for a short time. He did everything I wanted and showed me undivided attention. This was short lived. I didn't mind stirring up jealousy and often did. I was lost and hurting and didn't mind if anyone else was lost and hurting with me. Around this time I not only was throwing parties, but also helping run the after-hours Club 508. There were ongoing parties after work held privately at homes or in the clubs. I was messed up 24/7. If I was awake, I was high. I remember one time after the club closed, there was an after party. I had been up so long I fell asleep on the couch at the club. Anyone could have robbed me or set me up for anything. Z found me and was so mad. I had been having sex with other guys there at the club, also, in the bathrooms. I was a huge mess. Of all the guys I was with, Z treated me the best. He did try to help me, but there was only going to be one man who was enough to help me and that was Jesus Christ himself.

I remember the owner of the club telling me when certain undercover people were there. I didn't understand how all these people knew different things. It was a sketchy world. On top of all the paranoia from the drugs, there were real things to be paranoid about! People were getting arrested and then setting up other people. Almost every week it was something new.

Looking back, the sheer madness of the situations I found myself in is hard to believe. I remember one time when I was high and wanted a vest to show off my new thin body. I drove in a blizzard from downtown Nashville to the south side to get the vest from my cousin! I remember there were hardly any cars on the interstate. Most people in Nashville knew just how bad the roads were. It took me hours to go the fifteen miles there and back. I also remember hours of my time were devoted to shopping during these years. When I say hours, I mean it. If there was a shirt I liked, I had to try on every color or design. When I was high on speed, I had no sense of time. I had this new thin body and wanted to always look my best at the club and at parties. I would spend hours high and trying on clothes in American Apparel and Urban Outfitters. Z hated going shopping with me because of me "getting stuck." He would usually let me go alone, but when I took too long, he would accuse me of cheating on him. My life was a mess. I was miserable and starting to have second thoughts about why I was with Z.

A friend had told me Z was HIV positive. I didn't believe it at first, but I sensed it as the relationship moved forward. Z didn't tell me himself for a long time. I remember one time he was cooking something and saying how good this was for him. I remember thinking maybe he was sick in some way. Why was this specific food good for him? I was high and didn't have to work, though, so I didn't care too much. I even had unprotected sex with him at times. Looking back, this seems absolutely insane, but I was strung out on the drugs—I didn't care. I only know that for some reason my body was never infected with the HIV virus.

I had a routine. I would wake up and smoke a cig first thing. Then I would hit the nine ball filled with speed before I even got out of bed. The third part of the routine was taking my morning dose of Xanax. If I had speed and no Xanax, I was very unhappy. My sole goal was to have those two items every day. Once I started smoking speed instead of snorting it, I was hooked. I loved to speedball, as they call it. Mixing the downers with the uppers.

My life flung deeper into a downward spiral. After a few months of living with Z, we split and I moved in with another friend. I was working at the club and doing parties, but the recession effects of 2008 were hitting the working people hard. People didn't have so much money for "designer" drugs and definitely not for after-hours club fees. The parties had fewer and fewer people. My life was quickly on the downward spiral. I was finding myself more paranoid like the others. I was thinking someone was coming to get me. Once a friend found me in my apartment with a knife. I am not sure what I was going to do, but that is the state he found me in.

I remember one evening getting a call from a friend who was the manager of the apartment community we lived in. He was the friend who had found me with the knife. He called to tell me and the girl I lived with that the police had received an anonymous call that we were selling drugs in the apartments. My roommate and I started throwing pipes and other drugs down the bathroom tub. We were scared. I thought, *They are going to come in, and we are done.* I was thinking my jail time was coming soon. I was so scared. However, they never knocked on our door. Whoever had called had probably been a drug addict themselves. They knew our names but hadn't given proper info of the apartment.

I give all glory to Jesus because, once again, I feel my destiny took over. The plans God had for me superseded Satan's multiple times in my life. For some reason, God didn't want me to have drug charges. The manager told the police if they didn't have a warrant, they could leave. They did leave, and nothing came of it. My friend L had been there with me earlier that day. I had told her to go ahead and leave as soon as we found out. She had and told me later the police had been knocking on several doors. We all couldn't believe it. None of us had been arrested. After this incident I was scared, very scared. I was paranoid and knew that all the people talking about snitches in the group was a reality.

I kept partying and doing tons of drugs, and the sexual experiences increased. I remember I liked several "straight" guys in the club scene. I would bring them home to my apartment and engage sexually with them. I would get them high and make my moves from there. I had my first encounter of real prostitution. I was so low on funds I did what I had only heard about. I decided I would perform sexually with a man for money. I called an older man I knew and told him I needed cash for a bill. If he would come, I would do whatever he wanted. I performed oral sex on him, and he gave me forty dollars.

Wow, forty dollars for that disgusting act. I just got high and forgot about it. It made me believe what the devil had lied to me about: sex and my body were worth cashing in. I didn't know how Jesus viewed me: priceless. For the Lord decided we were not worth silver or gold, but the death of his only begotten Son. You are worth so much! Please, please know this. Your body when you become a follower of Christ Jesus is the temple of the Holy Spirit. He paid for you. If you are new and a baby Christian, I urge you, if there is anything to abstain from, it is sexual immorality. If you can't do anything else right at the early baby stage, then just abstain from that! "Flee from sexual immorality. All other sins a person commits are outside the body, but whoever sins sexually, sins against their own body" (1 Corinthians 6:18, NIV). Your body has become the temple of the Holy Spirit, and I believe sex is one of the ultimate ways Satan and demons like to attach unclean spirits.

I have to tell about one of the times I felt I was going to change. It was after I had heard about my friend Jenny's murder of McNair and her suicide and before I started hard on the crystal meth. I was working for Jane and Normand Coke. Norman had been a pastor, and his brother, Harold, was also a pastor for the Methodist church. They were such kind and Godly men. They always treated me as Jeffrey, not as a "homosexual." They treated me kind and encouraged me to go back to college and pursue my dreams. Harold and I got especially close. He was more mobile than his brother, Norman, and he and I spent a lot of time together. When I was with them, I would mostly be sober, work for them, and listen to them pray and talk about the Lord. I never knew just how much of an impact they had on me as I now realize. I had never been close to my paternal grandfather, and my mother's father had died when she was young. Harold became like this grandfather figure to me.

During this time, I felt the Holy Spirit come around me more, and I started reading the word and trying to figure out how I could change my life. Satan saw this and knew it was not the direction he wanted me to go in. The Lord was leading me away from this lifestyle and from my friends and family involved in it. I couldn't figure out how to just leave them alone. My life was so engulfed with them. Before I could fully submit to the Lord, the devil came as he does, like a roaring lion. Soon after I contemplated change, crying alone with heartfelt prayers, the enemy had me entrenched with crystal meth addiction. Satan also opened the club life to me and the men who came with it. It is so important to know every time I was close to a breakthrough, the devil came pouncing hard. He knew he didn't want me to fully surrender my life to Christ. Satan even knows our personalities, and he knew when I decided to live for Christ, it would be all the way.

My birthday was coming up. It would be May 5, 2010. One of my closest friends in this scene had money to spare and told me he would get his friend at the local swingers club to host my private invite-only party with my own DJ. In the drug world, this was heaven. I would have my own DJ spinning all my favorite music. I made a list for him of all my favorite old and new songs, and he found them and made remixes for me.

I partied all week prior to my actual birthday-party night. I remember going out with an Italian guy who was new to the scene. He said he was heterosexual, but that had never stopped me before, and I had the drugs to coerce him. He drove me to his house and got ready. We went to a local gay bar. I will never forget how I wore my first see-through shirt. I was thin and in love with my new body. I walked out into a busy street in front of the gay club, and the Italian guy grabbed me before a car could hit me. I was so high I was out of control.

After days of partying, it was almost time for my big party. The partying was so heavy that week. Z and I were arguing heavily after I moved back in with him. I had come home that week with the Italian guy, and Z was not happy about it. I had brought him home to the loft we shared without hesitation. I had introduced him as a friend. Z had gone and got Gigi's cupcakes, my favorite, for my birthday. I was so selfish I don't even remember being thankful for that or anything he had done that week. Of course, I know our relationship was wrong and not what God wanted for me. I still look back, though, and see how hardened my heart had become toward others. All I could think about was pleasing myself. My drugs and sexual escapades with men were my life. If it didn't help my personal flesh feel good, then I didn't care about others. My birthday party was about to shock me.

The day of the party arrived. I had a new outfit and was ready to look my best and go to the event. I had hair extensions to keep my hair full. I liked the way it looked during this time. I was always so concerned with my hair in my selfish times. I remember flat-ironing my hair for hours when I was high and always trying to perfect it. I got more comments on my hair in those years than anything else. Vain as a peacock, I got in the car and went to the party, which would be held at Menages.

Menages was a local swingers club. I didn't know much about it except I had partied with the owners, a man from South Africa and his wife, A. A had never liked me, and I could tell. But she did like the drug dealers, and since they were my friends, she would put up with me. I remember only once ever going to Menages before this birthday party. You could literally feel the spirits in that place from the sexual perversion. There had been so much partner-swapping and other encounters there that I could cut the sexual atmosphere with a knife.

I had never been there when it was open for business. The time I had gone before my birthday party it was closed—just the owners and their friends. My birthday party was also closed to the public. The owners talked about the building being owned previously by the Catholic Church years before. The previous time I had been there, they were talking horribly about God, which is something my friends knew I didn't like. I never tried to outright mock God. Sometimes, even when I was high, I would always speak about God being real and my belief that Jesus was real. The owner was actually mocking Jesus, and I could feel her hatred for the Holy Spirit. Something in her and something around me were not liking each other, and it felt like a constant clash! She spoke such vile and sexual words involving Jesus. I should have never gone there again, but it was the spot paid for by drugs to have my private party.

The party had just begun, and a few people were coming in. My friend, the dealer who had paid A for the private use of the club, soon walked in. He had brought someone who had previously been close with A, and now they were no longer friends. A got upset, so she told my friend he couldn't bring this girl into the club. Since this girl was kicked out, all my friends left. My friend who had rented out the club then spread word for no one to show up. Since he was one of the main drug dealers, hardly anyone came to my party. I was there alone.

I was upset and cried. I left the party and decided to go to my friend's home. When I arrived upset, my friend was mad that I had even stayed at the club after he had left. He was mean to me at first, and then we all got high and proceeded to party. By the next morning, people were going to bed. I decided to leave because I was high and couldn't sleep. Someone had called me from the party scene. I had never trusted this person because I had heard he'd done some undercover police work. I didn't really know if he had or not. He called me and said he wanted to pick me up. I let him pick me up and went back to Menages with him.

It was light outside and in the early hours of the next morning. When I arrived in the club, there weren't many people there. Then, slowly, people starting coming in. These were people I had known had been arrested or in some way had helped get people busted. Someone I knew asked me to go to the bathroom and gave me the largest piece of crystal meth I had ever taken. I swallowed it, what we called taking a capsule. I had repeatedly said it was too much, but he had kept saying, "Take it," and I did. The people there wanted me high out of my mind where I would talk. They got me in a room and psychologically battered me. They asked me questions about my friend and his drug dealings. A was mad anytime I said her name when I was talking like she didn't want me to. I noticed this and said it on purpose a few times. I was being recorded. I could see the guy next to me on his little laptop getting messages and responding to them on an IM-type setup that took up the whole screen.

I went out of the office later, having finally made it out and paralyzed with fear. I remember another girl there also crying. There are times I don't remember coming in and out. I also remember sitting on the couch and seeing the most evil, sinister grin from A. She was happy I was in her domain. I could see the demons in her twisted, distorted face. I remember also seeing dark spirits moving all around that place. If you don't think demons will stay in areas specific for sexual sin, you are very wrong. The evil in that place was so vibrant it felt like one could reach out and touch it. I remember having been warned months ago about this place. Was this the hangout for material being gathered on people selling drugs? Were these the people who had sold out to police to bring their friends down with them? I remember several people in the scene not liking the owners of Menages and avoiding the area, but some of the people from the speed scene were there that morning all gathered together.

I went crazy. I knew they were setting up my friends, and I knew they were trying to do something to me. I even noticed A put something in my Coach bag. I remember leaving and a cop following the car. It never pulled us over, and when I made it back to Z's loft, I was such a mess. I was crying and hysterical. I dug through the bag and found drugs that were not mine. I also found a weird device rolled up in some material. I told Z all of what had happened. I flushed my phone and the drugs I had found. I then told Z to take the device downstairs and throw it away in the laundry-room trash can. He did so and tried to calm me down. If it was an audio device, I didn't want it in the apartment. They had probably thought I was going back to my friend's house and wanted audio for the case. Z asked what had happened to my hair. I had ripped out a majority of the extensions. I had done this all at the club, and no one had done anything but watch me. These were evil people with evil spirits who loved the psychological torment I was getting from them. I took a bunch of Xanax and passed out. The next morning, Z told me later he had gone back to find the audio device. It was gone.

I told some people my story, and my friends listened but didn't take me too seriously. Months later, my friend was arrested. Every time I escaped situations, I thought, *How is this possible?* I didn't know the Lord was saving me to do his will in my life. I was getting to a point where I couldn't stay in Tennessee anymore.

Me with my dad

My brother Caleb and I

*Me at club
(crystal meth years)*

*Me as Scarlet
(full body)*

Me as Scarlet (taken during suicidal time)

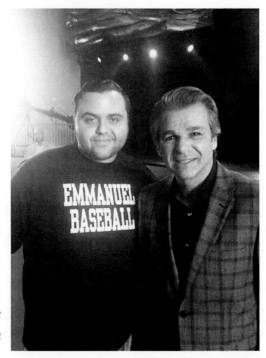

Finally getting to meet Jentezen Franklin

Meeting Phil Robertson sharing testimony in his hometown

Filming for the 700 Club

The first Freedom March, Washington, DC

CHAPTER FIVE

EMMANUEL COLLEGE AND QUESTIONS

I didn't know what to do. It felt like my life was collapsing. I needed to escape. I remembered my father had moved to Georgia and was coaching college baseball. He had implanted an idea in my mind the week of my birthday. He told me if I moved to Georgia with him, I could attend college there at Emmanuel for free because he was an employee. He and his wife, Leah, had been in Oklahoma visiting her parents with my younger stepbrother and little sister Bailey. On their way back, they could stop in Nashville to pick me up and I could go to Georgia with them. I would start a new life, and I would go back to college. I called my dad to tell him I would take him up on the offer.

I started college in August of 2010. I was so excited for this new life. I thought, *Here I am, away from drugs and the people I know.* When classes started, I quickly became friends with a girl who identified as homosexual. She introduced me to other girls she knew who played softball. I met other girls in Athens, Georgia, later in the school year and would party there. The University of Georgia is in

Athens, so there were bars and clubs in that city. The parties and guys were all around. I met a guy soon after moving to Georgia. He was typical of the kind of guy I liked. He wasn't feminine and had played baseball in high school. He was around my age of twenty-three, and I liked him a lot. I could escape with him from the Christian college and the people there and feel normal with him. The relationship ended quickly after a wild night of partying.

The college I went to was named Emmanuel College. It was started by the Pentecostal Holiness Church in 1919 in Franklin Springs, Georgia. It was a Christian college, and most of the people involved in it to this day are good Christians who want to help people. I had grown up in a Christian setting with Christian parents. But in my mind, I thought, *I got this. I can do it on my own.* My heart did melt some at Emmanuel College, and I was sobering up. I was sober on a daily basis for my freshman and sophomore years. I still drank on certain weekends, but during the week, I could think clearly. I would ponder on things the enemy had put into my life. My mind was so lost and desperate for answers. I started going to a Christian counselor on campus and explained some of the things I had gone through. It felt so good to get it out.

During this time, the beginning of my junior year of college, I felt I was making progress. The counselor was giving me a Christian perspective on some issues and sins that had plagued me. I didn't want to live the homosexual lifestyle, and I knew the enemy had used things from my childhood to make me believe this lie. I even at one point saw the Christian pastor on campus and had my counselor sum up the things I had gone through to try to help him understand my story. The pastor did try to help and showed me some material. I felt I was going in the right direction; I was seeking God. I had felt this way before when I had sought God when I worked for the Cokes in Nashville. The devil had stolen my walk with the Lord then, and he would soon be calculating how he would do so now. Soon the visits with the Christian counseling stopped.

I found out about a free walk-in clinic in the neighboring city. I decided to go there and spoke of some things that had bothered me. When I left the Christian counseling, it was exactly what the devil wanted. Soon after I saw the psychiatrist, he put me on Buspar and Celexa. I had a bad reaction to one of the drugs—I'm not sure which one, since he started me on two at once. I quit taking them and once again made the huge mistake of looking to my past to see what had made me feel well. I remembered! The feeling of Xanax to me was my heaven. It kept me calm, and my physical body felt so well when I was on it. I decided I would drive to Tennessee and see my old doctor.

As soon as I walked in the door, he prescribed just what I wanted. I came home and started taking the Xanax how he told me to, some in the morning and some in the evening. I felt great again! Before I could blink, though, I realized I was addicted once again to another drug. I once again was doing things on my own. I didn't want any more counseling, and since I was doing well in college, I didn't feel I needed it. I was at that state we all get in. I was thinking, *I am doing fine, and I can do this all by myself. I am doing great in school through MY work. I don't need anyone. I am going to do well and have a career of my own, make good money, and marry a man someday, and I won't need anybody.*

My senior year was pivotal for me. I noticed the more time went by, the more Xanax I needed to feel good the way I had before. I knew eventually it would get to be a massive amount of Xanax, and I wouldn't be able to take that much. I would hoard Xanax and get some off the streets to make sure I never ran out. The last semester was starting, and I had met a Christian professor who was teaching a biology class I needed. I hated biology and was so scared to take it. I put it off my entire college career until the last semester.

Something was different about this woman, though. Her name was Dr. Sherry Story. I knew she was different. I had seen her at basketball games and other times around campus. I could tell she knew something about me was different too. It wasn't that she knew I was living a homosexual lifestyle; this woman knew something about my pain. I could feel it in the spirit world.

I started her class in January, and it just so happens she also taught the photography yearbook elective class I was taking that semester. Some days I had her twice a day, and I could see she was funny and full of life. She never compromised her Christianity to our class. All jokes were clean, her spirit was clean, and her actions were something I didn't quite understand. I even had told my Christian counselor the fall before that I didn't want to become some stiff Christian. I didn't want to be someone who was never happy, always serious, and boring. This lady was a Christian but also full of energy and joy. My intellect wasn't understanding the situation.

I remember I started getting closer to her, and when an editor left the yearbook, she needed help. I then decided I would work for her when she asked our class for help. I didn't get paid much or have many hours, but I took it. It was almost as if I wanted to help her. When the job started, we talked a lot more. Someone had mentioned to me that she had made a video of what had happened in her life. I had to see it. I found it on YouTube, and it all clicked. She'd had things happen to her when she was young also. As I watched the video, tears streamed down my face. I knew what those things felt like, and I understood the innocence being taken away. But how was she happy now? She was happy and living life. She didn't hate anyone. I had never hated people and the things that had happened to me so much as being sad and feeling like a victim. She had described how she was full of Christ now. I had to talk to her about all this. When I asked her, she said she had a feeling some of those things had happened to me before. She told me how it took time, but the Lord had healed her. She told me she was whole now and knew her identity in Christ.

I was floored and I didn't understand. The world had shown me you couldn't be whole and satisfied ever. How was she so peaceful and happy with her life? I wondered, *Could Jesus really satisfy people today?* She had the peace and joy of the Lord—something I understand now. For people not living for God, it is not understandable to them.

Dr. Story was there for me at all times. I would talk to her about everything, and she always listened. We would go to lunches and talk for hours. My time at Emmanuel was coming to an end, and I knew I wouldn't have her every day. I was saddened by this. I felt like for the time, I could tell someone anything and everything and get a Christian perspective on it.

Graduation and awards night were coming up. My family from both sides were in town, and I was so ready to show them what I had accomplished. I was proud of my accomplishments. I mentioned God, but didn't give him the full glory for my accomplishments. Later, I would realize he was setting something up for later with my education.

The award ceremony night was one of the best nights of my life. I won the History Award from the history department and was also given awards for my academic works. I was so thrilled my family could see it. Graduation day was wonderful, and I had the degree in my hand. I was so proud of myself for sticking to it. It had been years since I had stuck to anything and actually accomplished it. On the outside, things seemed better, but inside I was still spiritually destitute.

After graduation, I went straight to Nashville, where my friends were planning a party for me. Everyone was completely drunk, but then I found out I had a surprise coming. A friend pulled me aside and told me the surprise was Y was coming. I was stunned; I had come full circle. I had been away, and now my past was showing back up. Y introduced his new boyfriend, whose name was Jeffrey. It was so ironic. Pretty soon me, my cousin, and Y were doing crystal meth bumps in the bathroom.

I stayed up that whole night. I drove to my brother's the next day for a Mother's Day barbecue. My younger brother had also been drunk and on speed with me the night before. He got drunk again the next day, and after spitting his food out on the table, decided to tell everyone we had gotten high. I was embarrassed and ignored it. Everyone just thought he was drunk and making a joke. (He has come so far and has a passionate zeal for Christ now! Just like his name, Caleb, he went into the Promised Land first, leading others to follow. He submitted to the Lord and had been living for him over a year before I did.)

Here I was now with a college degree and still having crystal meth weekends. Had I come full circle?

CHAPTER SIX

SCARLET, GRAD SCHOOL, AND THE PSYCH WARD

The summer after college graduation was pivotal to my next steps in life. I watched my niece and nephew in Murfreesboro, Tennessee, for my older brother. I reconnected with old friends, and I started drinking heavily. The Xanax wasn't working like it had previously, and the alcohol gave it a kick up. I was lonely, and lots of my other friends were married now or in serious relationships. I was not in any relationship and had gained a lot of weight in college, dragging what little self-esteem I had down. I had applied to graduate school and had been accepted to East Tennessee State University to gain a master's in history. I was excited to start, but nervous also. I was going to be alone in Johnson City, Tennessee. This was about five hours from my hometown and three and a half hours from where I had been in undergrad where my father lived. I knew in the upcoming months I would be far away from everyone and have lots of time alone.

I talked to Dr. Story about how I felt. I felt I could never change, and I was so not looking forward to losing my friends. My friends, so I thought, were a huge part of my world. Looking back now, I see my identity was so wrapped up in them and in how they saw me. Dr. Story asked me why I had even moved back to Tennessee. When I thought about it, there was no specific reason. I had just pushed to be back in the familiar, and Satan was going to use that for his next lie.

Being back home, I started hanging out with more of my old friends. Some of them lived homosexual lives, and some of them were heterosexual. All the heterosexual friends or acquaintances I had, of course, accepted everything I did. Then tragedy hit with one of my best friends, L.

L had been one of the closest people to me in my life. It was a friendship that is hard to describe. She was always there for me when I called, and I was always there for her. She had a lifelong addiction to benzodiazepines, the same as I had. She had taken Xanax and other pills and loved to drink. She is the friend I mentioned earlier in the story of almost getting busted for drugs in Nashville. We talked about our struggles all the time. L had a laugh that could light up the world. It was spontaneous, not like some people's. She only smiled and laughed when she meant it. If she didn't really feel the good emotion, it came off as a crooked frown.

Lots of her friends left her and didn't talk to her much as her addiction escalated. I never gave up on her, and I always tried to encourage her that she could overcome her drinking and pill problem. I remember the last time she called me. She seemed down because she had taken some benzos she had found from one of her family members. She had great guilt for this; her heart was so soft. She always felt remorse, which some people don't have. Most people would have been sorry they had been caught, but she was sorry that she had done it. That is hard to find in this world. She even mentioned she knew the devil was messing with her. I agreed and knew he was. I told her we just needed to pray and tried to uplift her spirit. She seemed well after a while, and we even laughed some.

I received a text the next day saying L had committed suicide that night after we talked. I was heartbroken—I couldn't believe it. I was so stunned. I had just talked to her.

Just a few days later, it was time for her memorial. She had been cremated, which I didn't know until I got to the funeral. Her mother knew how close we were and asked me to be an honorary pallbearer. I said yes, of course. When I arrived, there was no physical body. I couldn't see her as I had done with Josh and Aunt Carol. I was hurting but couldn't grieve in my own way. I still to this day don't like cremations. To me, she had just been there, and now she was gone. I had just talked to her, and now there was no body. All I saw were pictures of her and memorial-type things, but she wasn't there. I was devastated.

The funeral occurred, and the family ate together afterward. A friend and I had ridden together, so we left after the service. We played "Bitter Sweet Symphony." That song reminded me of L. I was so sad. I think, in a way, I needed something new. Death was so final to me. It was too much at this point. I listened finally to that lie Satan had always thrown at me, that I was more female, to try to transform my life. All my life, everything had failed, and this was another catalyst for me to transform my life even more.

Later that summer, I would do my first drag show. My cousin who had done drag shows and I had always been close. When I came out as gay, he immediately took me under his wing. I had watched him do drag and been around him getting ready, but I had never done it myself.

My opportunity came when my brother was taking his family on vacation. I would have his house to myself. I don't even remember exactly what I felt or what I was thinking, but somehow I wound up using my sister-in-law's extensions as a hair piece over my own hair, and I did my own makeup. I had watched so many girlfriends of mine do their makeup and hair, I figured I could do my own.

Once I shaved and did the foundation, powder, and eyes, I decided to put the hair on. I took photos and sent them to a friend. She was a model, and I wanted her opinion on how I looked as female. She was also pretty honest about things to me. She would really tell me her opinion. Because of my weight, I didn't really have an Adam's apple, and with the makeup and my round face, you couldn't tell so much that I was male in the photos. She replied that I looked great, like a "real girl." I never did makeup eccentric or drag, as they call it. I just did a common "girl" look.

The next night an old friend of mine—a guy from my drug days long ago—came over. I was dressed as Scarlet, the name I went by. He brought some speed, and we took some bumps and hung out. He ate the bulk of it (parachuting), and we were both high. He had never seen me like this, and later we had sexual encounters. Now, I'd had sexual encounters before with this guy, but I could tell he liked this. It was different. I knew he had a girlfriend and baby, but I didn't care. I was selfish and doing exactly what I wanted. I felt pretty as Scarlet, less self-conscious. I thought, *Maybe this is what I have been looking for. Maybe this is the missing link to my happiness. Maybe I have not been successful as a gay male and I always felt like a woman. I identify with women; maybe this is who I really am.*

Some days or weeks afterward, I thought, *I want to do a*

drag show. There was a new club in Murfreesboro that had drag shows, and I wanted to be a part of it. I talked to people there and told them I could bring a crowd.

I started preparing for the drag show. I wanted everything to be perfect. I wanted to dazzle the crowd and make my appearance before my friends. This was going to be glory to me and what I could do. I practiced makeup and different hairstyles. I pushed my chest up as high as I could and changed my body with padding to try to figure out what looked good. I will never forget the booties I wore that night. I could barely walk in them!

I delivered my promise to the club that I would bring the crowd. So many people came and supported me. It blew my mind. The center stage was me, and I was what the people had come to see. It was all about me, and I could feel the energy of the crowd. Little did I know, Satan and his demons had planted a seed that was rooted deep in me. I had never fully fit in with other gay men. I was tall and broad no matter how thin I was. I was never going to fit in with that twinkie look my friends had. This let me fit in. I felt like a tall, bigger, pretty woman. I noticed immediately I got more attention from the males who openly liked transsexual girls. I could also tell I could spark an interest from guys who weren't so sure about their sexuality. This was a Jezebel spirit, though I didn't know it at that time. I could make males do things they usually wouldn't, and the spirits around me were using me to entice and seduce men.

I played around with becoming Scarlet and started meeting men online. Craigslist is where I went most of the time. I had sexual encounters but focused most of my time on my first year of graduate school. I eventually made a Facebook for my alter ego. Scarlet Diaz Andrews was the name I chose. That summer after my first year of grad school, I dressed a lot more. I had told some family and didn't care if they knew or not. I was hurting a lot after that first year.

With my newfound way of life, I embraced myself as Scarlet. I thought it was great. The year before, the show director had even asked me about being on cast as one of the "showgirls" of the club I had performed at. I told the club manager no, because I was going to grad school. That club eventually closed a few months after I performed. The next summer, I had my Scarlet Facebook page set up and was living my life as Scarlet. I did more shows and started to have a name around the local area. I did shows in smaller towns, and I liked it that way. I didn't have the pressure of ever trying to make a perfect show like the drag queens in Nashville who worked at bigger clubs. First of all, there was no way I could have. That summer is when the drinking started heavily. I had to do something to make me feel okay with what I was doing. A lot of queens use crystal meth, marijuana, alcohol, or prescription drugs to help them cope. Now, I know someone will say there is a drag queen or transsexual out there who is sober all the time, and I am sure there are some, but trust me—they are not the majority.

The new school year began. I was now in my last and final year of graduate school. I was so close to completing my extended education and having a master's degree to go along with my bachelor's. I was so excited for the beginning of my new life after this school year was over. I had big dreams and wanted to move to any big city. I thought my life was soon to begin, and I saw myself as Scarlet. I wanted to live as a woman and would do anything to do so. I told my psychologist, who was homosexual, that I wanted to live as a woman. I also told my new psychiatrist I wanted to live as a woman. Both of them thought I was transgendered, and the psychiatrist even ruled me as having gender dysphoria. It had been so easy—I told them I felt comfortable as a woman, and everyone in the medical profession had said I was a woman. I had clothes now, along with wigs, jewelry, makeup, and shoes. I did makeup almost every other day and started doing different hairstyles. It took time, but I got better at accentuating my chest and padding to have more of a curvy figure.

The promiscuous sex really started that semester. I could not be Scarlet or be with men without being drunk. I would drink while I got ready. Drinking was a huge part of my life dressing as Scarlet. I would get on Craigslist and make ads and start pouring the drinks. I started having sex with a number of men. It was almost every other day I would have a drunken hookup. I would be so hungover the next day. I even started going out as Scarlet to restaurants and "straight" bars. I started meeting men out. I was an easy sexual toy to these men. I was having sex with different men every week. Sometimes, when I was on drunk binges, I would have sexual encounters with three or four guys a day. My life seemed hopeless unless I had Scarlet and the men to make me feel something. I thought, *Once I fully transition into Scarlet, then I will be happy.* Then I met a guy.

I met Josh around September of 2015. He was a country guy who was into dating transgender women. I remember when I met him, I wanted to have a relationship with him. I felt so attracted to him. Josh had a previous relationship with a drag queen from the town I lived in. I knew he had dated this other guy and they had eventually lived together. Josh described to me one day that when they had lived together, he never touched or had sexual relations with this man without him being dressed. So I did that just to keep his attention. I never let Josh see me not as Scarlet. It was a full-time job. I had to shave all the time and keep makeup in the house and ready for when Josh would come over. I had to keep lots of new outfits to keep his interest. He told me I was beautiful and made me think he was falling for me.

One weekend, we were supposed to go camping. I was excited and nervous. I had never been to his property where he lived. His family had a farm and land. I got drunk while I waited on him. He was running late and eventually told me he wasn't coming. I was so mad. I was angry and hurt. Immediately I felt rejection because that is what I seemed to always feel from men. They didn't mind having sex with me, but I longed to spend more time with them and fall in love with them. Josh had spent time with me and made me feel special. He made me feel like he truly loved me.

When the thought came that this could be ending, I lost it. I threw stuff in my apartment and broke things. I screamed and cried. I thought about hurting myself, but I knew I didn't want to. I decided I needed to call for help. When I did, I said I had thoughts of killing myself. I didn't know what was going to happen, but I did know I needed help. I needed it desperately. Part of me that night did want to commit suicide, and part of me just wanted to scream out for help.

When the campus police came, they escorted me out. The police officer was nice to me, but I didn't want to talk.

There was a fire truck and ambulance and police cars outside my hallway as I moved from the police car to the ambulance. I was taken to the psychiatric ward of the hospital. I was given my own room there, and I was analyzed by some medical personnel. I remember sitting in that room drunk and alone. I remember a girl from school coming to check on me. I guess the school sends someone every time there is a student checked in to the hospital. She talked to me and tried to calm me down, but I was so combative and mean to the nurses and doctors.

Once I was admitted, they decided I would go to Woodridge mental facility. It was literally across the road. I had to stay in the hospital for two days. I was drunk the first night and wanted them to let me smoke, but they wouldn't. On the second day, I decided I would outsmart them. Bruce Jenner had just made the public transition into Caitlyn. I knew with all the media and transgender-rights issues going on, they would let me stay in the hospital as Scarlet. The nurse let me do my makeup every day. I realized the cigs I had brought into the hospital were in the same bag. I sneaked them out when the nurse wasn't looking. I used her weakness of being overly friendly to get the cigs. I wasn't in my right mind, I remember that. I was different at the hospital—very mean—and that is not like my real, God-given personality. I lit up and smoked two cigs in my room. I then peeked through the glass window. You could tell the nurse was looking around. I opened the door and grinned and told her I had smoked in my room. I hope to this day I did not get her in trouble. I remember afterward I gave her the cigs back and told her I was sorry but that I had to smoke. Two cops who worked at the hospital came in and were mad I had smoked in the hospital. I was rude to them also, and when one didn't call me ma'am, I yelled at him. This was not my spirit talking, but this hurt, deceitful person I had become. I had no care for others. There were gas pipes that ran throughout the ceilings, and I had put everyone there in jeopardy by smoking. I was so selfish. I remember the day they told me I was finally going to leave the hospital to go to Woodridge. I was just happy to get a new setting.

They put me in a secured van, and I only saw sunlight for a couple of seconds. Anyone who has spent days away from seeing the outside knows this feeling. I remember being taken directly to the van and then the van being driven to the door of the mental hospital. When I got in the door, I was treated like a criminal. I understand this was for their protection, because hospitals like that deal with so many people. I was taken into this old, 1950s-looking room with green tiles. I was told to strip and take off all my clothes. I was told they had to check all the bras and padding I had for my hip and buttock shape. After they inspected the padding, they told me I wouldn't be able to use it. They took the bras and said they had to wash them and remove all wiring. I had to stand there naked and lift my hands. They inspected my body with the cough search. It was three women, and I felt mortified. I felt alone and scared in that place, and I knew nothing of what to expect. I don't even remember getting moved to the floor where I was moved to.

Everything was discombobulated and weird at the hospital. I couldn't have gotten out even if they had opened the doors to my hall, because I didn't know where anything was. It still is strange looking back and thinking about it. When I walked in, everybody looked at me. The men did double takes. Then they came closer, like predators about to pounce. I wore a long wig with a short, layered wig over it. It looked like really long hair with layers. They took the long wig and said the pieces in it weren't allowed. So all I had was the short, thin top layering. I told them they could cut all pieces out of the long wig so I could wear all the hair to make myself seem more attractive. It shows you my priorities—I was literally thinking about hair in a mental hospital! I was obsessed with being Scarlet. I know now there were spirits controlling me then.

The first girl I noticed had dark hair and bright-red lipstick. She came and talked to me and was friendly. I will call her G. I asked her if we could wear lipstick, because her lips were obviously painted. She said no, she had just gotten there, and that's why she had lipstick on. She continued talking to me, and we hit it off. She reminded me of L, whom I had just lost.

G was in the front of the line for vitals that night. We had to line up and then sit in front of the line where the blood-pressure machine was. The nurses would take your blood pressure and then your temperature. G was crying. My heart went out to her. I asked one of the nurses why she was crying. They said it was her first night and she was upset. That night, I went into the room they had for me. I remember it was cold. It had a stone floor and two twin-size beds. There was a Bible on the table. I didn't even want to read it. I didn't believe in anything but myself at that point. A man was walking down the hall peering in my room the whole time. I felt uncomfortable, but eventually I went to sleep. Before I could fall asleep, someone peered in the room and shined a flashlight on me to make sure I was in bed. I thought, *Of course I am in bed, people, where would I go?* This ward they put me in was the lowest-watched ward. I remember it was called Laurel Ward. This was for people they didn't feel they had to watch too closely. To be clear, we were still locked up with absolutely no control and no way to get out. There were men and women in this ward. Most people had roommates, but I always had my own room while I was there.

The next morning, I woke to a not-so-great breakfast. I picked at it and ate what I could. I found out that day there were also juice cups in the fridge in the common area. I went there, and the cable was on. I sat down and eventually saw G, and we started talking. We hit it off again and stayed together anytime we could be together. We had meetings about anger and how to do things when we're sad or upset. It seemed all in good conscience, but without Christ, you just keep doing those things. Several of the people in Woodridge I met had been there before. I remember G and I discussing life. We had decided we needed sun and asked when our day for the courtyard would be. I remember a picture of a sun painted on one of the roof tiles. G made me laugh so hard. She said, "That is just torture."

"What?" I asked.

"The sun painted on the roof tile," she replied. She told the nurses we needed to see outside and the sun. The nurses replied that our recreation time would come.

They finally took us outside one day. Someone told us of a man who did meditation. Somehow G and I got out there around the same time as this man, and he led us through meditation. When lost people are searching for something, they will think anything works. I went for it, but no inner strength came through, only my own ideas. At the end of it, nothing changed.

G and I stayed close. We started hanging out with another older lady and a younger guy who were also in our ward. One day while coloring (yes, we colored), we all talked about what had happened and why we were there. The younger guy told us about staying up on speed and how he had freaked out on a friend. The older lady told us about her depression and how when she had been younger, the father of her daughter had made her think he loved her. He had invited a bunch of friends over one day. The man and all his friends had raped her. The man she loved had watched while multiple men had sex with her. I couldn't believe all the things I was hearing. What was going on? This was crazy! I realized I wasn't alone in my own messed-up life. A lot of people were hurting, and some of them didn't even want to live!

Then G told me why she was there. She had been a teacher. She was well educated and also had a master's degree. She had been so distraught mentally that she had planned to kill herself when she got home from school. She planned it out and had the pills ready for when she got home. Her husband eventually knew something was going on, and when asked she told him. He notified the authorities, and she got help and got sent to Woodridge. All I could think of was L. G reminded me of L, and now she was telling me she had planned suicide. I was devastated for my new friend.

Life felt surreal, but very real, all around me there. Life and the brink of death, or the spirit of death, were all around. When I finally met the doctor, I talked him into thinking it was just me throwing a fit. He decided I should go home since I was in graduate school, so I could continue my studies. I got out and immediately went to my apartment. I remember thinking, *Wow, what have I just experienced?* I still remember getting to leave and taking off the leggings they had given me and putting on my boots and skirt. The first thing I did before I even walked out the door was fix my lips. G saw me putting my lipstick on and yelled, "Bye, Scarlet, I am going to miss you!" I have not seen her since that day and have talked to her only a couple of times since I got out. The last time I tried to call her, which was around two years ago now, I got no response. I no longer have her number. I hope she is okay.

I had called Josh in the mental ward and semi told him what happened. Surprisingly, he wanted to see me. He tried to make me feel okay and said he understood. He'd had some mental episodes himself. I hadn't known all of this before. I thought, *Great, both of us can try to understand each other's crazy.* We stayed together another month after I got out, but it didn't work. I was always jealous of him, or we couldn't get along because of my horrible drinking problem. I was devastated when he left. He had finally told me he loved me before Halloween, and I was so excited. I thought we were really going to be together. We got drunk and hung out with a guy I knew from graduate school on Halloween night. I acted crazy and took off walking in a corset with a skirt and five-inch heels down a highway. When I saw the hill I was going to have to climb in those shoes, I turned right back around.

I got a ride back with Josh, and we finally calmed down at the apartment. We decided after the horrible fight earlier that evening, we would stay in for Halloween. We actually got along the rest of the night, and it was one of the better times we had. The next morning, when he got up, he stayed awhile and lingered around the house. He left, and I never saw him again. The preparation of guys coming into my life and leaving suddenly had started from the first guy, X. This relationship with Josh had hurt me super deep, though. I thought I had fully found someone who would be there for me. I thought I had someone who would accept me for who I thought I was.

When Josh left, I gave up on the relationship aspect of the men I was with. I did meet one older man who started to like me and was more stable and wanted to possibly pay for some of my male-to-female body surgeries, but he left also. After Josh left, I was on Craigslist all the time putting out ads. I had sexual encounters with so many men, I don't even know the number. I remember one guy I met wanting to pimp me out. I agreed and had sexual encounters with the men he brought over. One literally had no money and left five dollars. I remember how lonely some of them were. Some would talk before sexual encounters, and some didn't even have sex with me. They just hung out. A lot of these guys were lonely themselves. I was at the lowest point of my life.

I was hurt. Satan had bombarded my mind with all the sex and love I yearned for from men. I wanted attention from men, and I found this attention through sex. The guilt continued to plague me. I thought about dying all the time. If God wasn't real, then death would be a great outcome. I would just be dead in the ground. The late-night and early-morning calls to my father began. I would call him drunk and say I wanted to die or commit suicide. I was so unhappy with my life and all the people in it. I felt like I was screaming and no one could hear me. Most friends said it was the weaning off anxiety meds and didn't pay attention to the spirit realm. By the end of my second year of graduate school, I had weaned off a lot of the benzodiazepines and was on a small dose. My internal hurt was hard to deal with now, especially at the low dose of the medicines that were making me numb to everything.

I was also counting the cost of possibly not seeing certain family if I chose to go through with the surgeries and transition fully to Scarlet. Was it worth it to change my body and risk my father never wanting to see me again? Would he also not let me see my little sister ever again? Would I be allowed to come as Scarlet to family functions on both sides of the family? I counted the costs in my mind and still decided it would be better to lose family and become Scarlet. This deception of becoming something I was not had taken full control over my mind.

During this time, the Lord was using a preacher to speak into my life. I had visited this man's church years ago. His name was Jentezen Franklin. I was beginning to question things about my life and why I felt such darkness and depression. Since I was living as Scarlet, I didn't feel comfortable going to church, but Pastor Franklin came on television and had several videos on YouTube. I started watching him. I would listen to his sermons and feel conviction at times. Questions were arising about my sexual appetite and how selfish and vindictive I had become. I even remember thinking of setting up a married lawyer I was having an affair with and exposing him to his wife for financial gain. As low as things were getting, I knew there had to be more to life. It was around this time I had my first supernatural encounter with God.

I will never forget the night the encounter occurred. I was in my apartment alone that night. It was late at night, and I was depressed. I just collapsed on the bed and cried out. I basically my whole life believed there may be a God, and when I cried out, I remember thinking, *He may be listening, but who knows?*

I said, "God, I know that people live for you—not just go to church on Sunday, but something happened and their life was transformed—but will I ever live for you?" I felt like I was a million miles away from the little boy I was who believed in God.

As I cried and had thoughts running through my mind, suddenly everything went silent in my mind and I heard a voice say, "Yes, you will live for me."

I was shocked. I had to collect myself. Did the God who created heaven and earth just speak to me? Why did I just know it was God? Why had my thoughts bowed down in silence when he spoke?

God comforted me that night with that simple statement. My life, to me, seemed about as far as one could be from God. God knew the beginning from the end, though, and he knew eventually I would choose him. That evening he had planted a mustard seed of hope within my spirit. After a couple days, I suppressed the experience.

After the end of my second year of graduate school, I decided to move back to Nashville. I moved in with a friend from high school. This friend and our third roommate were both living trans lives. They both were females who went by the pronouns he or them. They both supported my life as a woman. I got a job waiting tables in downtown Nashville. I met several girls and some guys I befriended at the restaurant I worked at, where I noticed a dishwasher who looked like a country music star. I found him attractive and decided to throw out the bait. I told him about my lifestyle, and he was willing to hang out. I blew so much money one night partying with him. We were both drunk, and I knew what I wanted at the end of the night. The guy had sexual relations with me that night. After it was done, I took him home the next morning. The devil knows when you are willing to help lead someone else in sin, and I was. I had tricked so many men into trying the twisted sex I presented. It was a lie, and nothing about it was real. Satan could twist men into lust through the alcohol and through my warped perception of female traits. Once again, after it was done, we never talked to each other again.

The last night of my life in Nashville was absurd. I met a guy online and had him meet me for drinks. Once we met up, the liquor started pouring. I had talked to an old friend from my previous drug days. He had quit using speed, but now drank heavily. I decided me and the guy I was with would stop by his house for drinks. I was drunk before I left my house. When we arrived, all of us began drinking. Before long, I was extremely drunk. I woke up the next morning very hungover. My friend had texted me saying he needed me to call him immediately, so I called him right away and he told me about the night before. I had apparently tried to fight with the guy who had brought me over. My friend had then called an Uber for me. He could track the Uber on his phone and showed me I had gone to the gas station by his house. This was the same gas station where I had been picked up by my father six years previously when I had been on speed and decided to leave with him to attend college in Georgia. Had I come full circle?

My friend told me he had paid the driver to take me home and gave my address. The driver told my friend she had called the cops on me after I had asked to go to the store. I vaguely started remembering several cops coming to the store. One had taken me home in the back of his car. I had a couple of weeks earlier been pulled over drunk in Nashville going the wrong way down a one-way street. The cops on both nights never even wrote me a ticket! Had I pushed my "luck"? Was it time for me to leave Nashville?

I then remembered I had called my father the night before. He was on his way to get me.

I met my father in Murfreesboro at a Cracker Barrel. I arrived but could barely eat. It was hot that day, and I was hungover. I'll never forget how the mascara and eyeliner melted and smudged on my eyes. I was so happy to see him. I was so ready to go home with him to Georgia. We went to Manchester to see my brother Caleb and stay the night with him. Caleb was angry with me and tired of all the late-night calls. I had apparently called him too and not been so nice. Caleb had been living as a Christian, and something in me knew I wanted to be saved and that it was for me. I just wasn't ready to actually live for the Lord. I knew what that would involve: me losing the life I wanted to live.

Caleb prayed for me and rebuked strongholds. I slept well that night being near my brother and father. They were both people I have always had an unbreakable bond with. I remember thinking, when Caleb prayed and put anointed oil on me, that some demons were probably going to scream and fly out. I didn't know much about the spiritual realm and if it happened that way. I know now something shifted in those days around these events. The Lord was using multiple things to move me in a new direction.

Chapter Seven

Creation, Prophets, and Facebook Live

I was finally going to see about living a different life. I moved to Georgia with my dad. There I would be living with my father, my sister Bailey, and my stepmother, Leah. I fought God so hard during this point. He was, however, leading me slowly forward. God is patient, and he was showing me this. He wanted me, but all of me. The first thing that went was all my jewelry, women's clothing, and shoes. It was in a suitcase, and I had decided it needed to go. I didn't fully understand everything at that point, but the Lord was helping my brain to make a decision. I took the suitcase full of my life as Scarlet and threw it in a local dumpster. Had I really just thrown away my life as Scarlet? Becoming Scarlet had been the end goal of my life. I had seen psychologists and psychiatrists and moved my life into a direction to one day have male-to-female surgeries. The very thing I had worked so hard to become seemed so easy to throw away. Something was changing rapidly.

 The second thing that happened was letting go fully of the anxiety pills. I was then on a very low dose of Valium. I decided no more weaning off, since the dose I had was low anyway. I took the plunge and jumped off. Each day was painful and different. Some days were just plain weird. Then I decided the depression and anxiety medicine Lexapro had to go. I went from 20 mg to 10 mg a day. It also brought hard days, and I had to learn to deal with anxiety in other manners. Now I know the Lord "was pierced for our transgressions, he was crushed for our iniquities; the punishment that brought us peace was on him, and by his wounds we are healed" (Isaiah 53:5, NIV). Jesus paid for my peace by letting my punishment rest upon himself. I don't think in any way it was fair for him to take on my punishment, but I also learned later to not lean on my own understanding. God's ways are higher than ours. Now I receive that he paid for it, and I can have peace without pills and alcohol.

One day, my father and I got in a heated debate. I told him I didn't even know if I believed in God anymore. I honestly, in my depraved mind, didn't know. I was searching every day for proof God wasn't real. Satan was lying to me, and I was buying it. I would look up videos online and read articles. Surely these renowned scientists and others all knew the truth. Most of them never acknowledged God or Jesus. These people professed evolution. Another idea I picked up from these professors and scientists was that we as humans had become our own God! Mankind doesn't naturally like to even notice God. Man wants to uplift their works, not the creator who made them! Then the Lord drew me to a video. It helped in answering a lot of questions I had about God and creation and proved things I needed to understand. The Lord had to lay a foundation for creation, which he did with his word and videos from Christian scientists.

That summer in 2016, the Lord stripped everything the

LGBTQ had told me about God, and all my church background also. It was like he wanted to lay the foundation of who he was. There were even nights I would cry because I could feel God and Satan battling in my mind. Satan would come telling me God wasn't real and the Bible was fake. I even remember one night saying, *God, I can't think anymore about creation. Please let me fall asleep!* God answered my prayers and gave me peace that night. I was going through a battle of my intellect, thinking it was higher than God. Now I know he wanted a solid foundation, for if the foundation is not built by Jesus and on Jesus, it will crumble. The Lord was basically telling me at this point, "I have shown you, now will you follow?"

I began to follow Jesus, and things changed. As time went on, the Lord was changing me. I accepted Christ Jesus, and I had a yearning to be baptized again. I was baptized by my dad and his friend Darren in South Carolina's Lake Keowee. Soon after this, my father asked me to go with him to a Sunday service at his friend Darren's church in South Carolina. It was a Pentecostal church, and they were having an evangelist from Ireland coming to speak. I agreed to go, and we went that Sunday morning.

I didn't exactly know why the evangelist was there or what he would talk about, but as he began preaching, I listened. I remember during worship there was a point when I couldn't stand up for long. I didn't know if this was the Holy Spirit or the medicine withdrawal, but something was happening. After the service, the Irish man had his wife pray for healing over people, and he gave prophetic words. I almost didn't go up to the front for prayer, but I knew I needed to. I told my dad I would go at the end. I remember thinking to myself, *If he says one thing wrong, it will crumble everything you have established, God!*

At the end of the service, I went up with my father. It was incredible! The man told me I had dreams, so many dreams it could break a millionaire! That was one of my problems. One day I wanted to be a teacher, another day a lawyer, another a writer, another day thinking about opening a business. I had the right heart, and all my dreams were mostly about helping people. He told me the Lord was going to open the right doors for me to do what he wanted me to do. Then the man prophesied that my intellect would go under God and he would show me things! I couldn't believe it! How did this man know about my aimless thinking every day when the evil and good were battling in my mind about creation and other things pertaining to God? It was like this man knew about my many nights asking God to please let me quit battling with Satan over whether he was real. The spiritual warfare during those nights had been tormenting and heavy!

Then the prophet told me I would have platforms open for me quickly and that it wouldn't take long. I was astonished! The Lord had just recently put a burning on my heart that one day I would be sharing my story and helping others. When he said platforms would open soon, I knew I had to finally submit to God fully. The Holy Spirit spoke through that man, and I am grateful for his obedience in doing and saying what the Lord Jehovah wanted him to speak forth. When I walked out of the church building, the Holy Spirit starting showing me that I needed to make a video cutting ties with everything from my past. He was asking me to lose even more of my life.

The video was hard for me to make. Up until that point, everything that was happening spiritually in my life was secretive. I wasn't telling my close friends or other family members I was close with. Now the Holy Spirit was wanting me to make a video and publicly renounce homosexuality and Scarlet. He also wanted me to share about my life and other struggles I had been through. In my mind, this was too much for him to ask of me at this time.

I fought the Lord on this. I didn't want to speak the truth. I didn't want to lose my friends. I didn't want to lose some family who would disagree with the truth. If I made the video, I knew several would have some negative comments about it and some would leave me. The Lord showed me one day who would leave of my friends. He also told me it wasn't so much to do with me, but that they had their hearts hardened to him. He showed me I would have to lose them and lose that part of my life. It was a hard pill for me to swallow.

I put it off for some time, but then on August 16, 2016, I made the video. I went to Dr. Story's office, who had been there through it all. I told her I needed to go live but didn't have the newest iPhone to do it on. She let me use her phone. I could see the excitement on her face. She knew that what I was about to do was going to be powerful and life changing. I made the video and discussed my life. I also stated I didn't want to be part of the homosexual lifestyle and would be cutting ties with all things involved with it. While I was making the video, I could feel good and evil fighting outside the door.

The day the video was made, my life really changed. My old life was over. It felt as if the weight of the world was lifted off me! I felt born again, truly like a new creation. After that video, I felt such joy and peace. From that day forward, the Bible became alive to me; it was no longer just a historical book with rules and regulations. I would begin to lose a lot of friends, something that weeks before seemed unimaginable. It was as if suddenly I had the grace to lose them. Following Jesus just seemed more important. He had sacrificed so much for me. He had laid down his perfect life for me. Could I not lose some friends? Some of the friends I lost felt like baggage being cut off, and some I still miss to this day. Jesus tells us that blessed are those who lose family and others for his sake. If you have ever been left out of friend/family functions because of your belief in Christ, then let this scripture encourage you right now: "If you are reproached for the name of Christ, blessed are you, for the Spirit of glory and of God rests upon you. On their part he is blasphemed, but on your part he is glorified" (1 Peter 4:14, NIV). I knew I had to move forward with God's plan for my life, and not everyone was coming with me.

I know now the Lord has so much in store for my future. I have much responsibility for my life and my future. I have to be a shining example of what Christ can do and how he can use anyone no matter their past. I want to help people move out of sexual sin and move into their identity in Christ. You see, you are not the identity the devil makes you think you are. Jesus can wash away your sins, he can make you whole, he can show you that you have identity through him! It is not what others say you are, but what Jesus claims you are.

Jesus died for us! Let that sink in. Jesus died for you and me on that cross with all sin on him! He had never sinned and didn't deserve to taste death, but he did. Satan is so mad at God's sacrifice for us humans. God loves us so much and hates when we push him away. If you really think about it, what happens when we do things our way? It usually turns out a mess. There are millions of "successful" people in the world, and those who don't have Christ are unhappy! They may look happy on the outside and play pretend on Facebook, at social functions, and even at church, but if they don't truly know Christ and have a relationship with him, I can guarantee they are unhappy people inside. Something is missing for them, but it is right there with Jesus if they would follow him.

I love each and every person reading this, not from my personal self but through Christ's love. I want everyone to know Christ and get into heaven. Why would you want to be separated from God forever? People reading this need to know that voice pulling on your heart is the Holy Spirit. He is leading you now to repentance. Follow it and submit to the Lord. He can use you in his mighty way to help others, but most importantly he wants a relationship with you. 2 Peter 3:9 (NIV) states, "The Lord is not slow in keeping his promise, as some understand slowness. Instead he is patient with you, not wanting anyone to perish, but everyone to come to repentance." From the beginning, mankind was created to be in relationship with God. Check out Genesis and find out how it was all supposed to be before sin entered the world. My story is only one, and so many others out there have important stories also!

God has chosen you, now listen and follow him. You too can become a fisher of man's soul and walk out your destiny through Christ Jesus that he had for you before the foundation of the world! He made a way for you thousands of years ago in Jerusalem, when he sent Jesus to handle the issue of sin. Look what God did for us: "For God so loved the world that he gave his only begotten son that whosoever believes in him shall have eternal life." You can be back in relationship and fellowship with God by putting your faith in Jesus Christ. Just talk to him right where you are at. It doesn't have to be at a church. Just speak to him and tell him you are sorry for your sin and you want a new heart from him. Now follow him and get in the word of God and see what he wants you to do and how he wants you to live. Ask for his Holy Spirit to fill you and give you grace to walk out this life. The Holy Spirit will come and fill you and teach you all things of Jesus. You will be a new creation, and he will lead you and guide you into a brand-new life! Not every day will be perfect, but he will be with you, guiding you and teaching you. Make the decision today, for you are not promised tomorrow!

CHAPTER EIGHT

THE SUPERNATURAL

The dream I described at the beginning of this book followed me my entire life. From a little boy, the Lord had a plan for me and Satan wanted it destroyed. I thought I would never understand the dream, and that possibly, even one day, I would get a dream interpreter through Christ to explain it to me.

One day, the Holy Spirit laid on my heart the interpretation. I was watching Jentezen Franklin preach. Free Chapel is my home church, but I didn't always get to visit because of distance, so on some days I would watch through internet sources. He preached on Elijah. Now, for some time I had understood the two men in my dream were Elijah and Moses. The Lord then delivered to me, through the Holy Spirit, the interpretation of my dream. Elijah represented a prophetic call on my life. In the Bible, Elijah called out to the Lord and asked to just die. I had gotten to that state in my own life. The Lord revealed to me Jezebel and the spirit of Jezebel, which had come to destroy my life. The spirit was a controlling-of-men attitude. I had been afflicted with this spirit and had controlled men through sex. It had eaten at my peace and joy until I was at the point Elijah got to when he fled and was alone. That spirit was powerful and deceptive. It wanted to destroy Elijah and what he needed to do for the Lord. Satan had hoped that spirit would destroy me also. Do not for one second think that the Jezebel spirit cannot come upon a man, for demons have no respect for gender.

Moses was revealed to me also. Moses led his people out of bondage and slavery. The Lord revealed to me I would, through his power, help take people out of sexual bondage and slavery. The chains would be broken off many! This is why the bear, representing Satan, came into my dream mad and angry. He didn't want what I was going to do for the Lord to be fulfilled.

Knowing this dream is powerful. I never knew it before, but it shows me my responsibility for the kingdom of Christ and what I have to do now! There is no turning back, but only growth as a Christian and moving forward. I am not perfect by any means. Nobody is; only Christ lived without sin. I am learning even through my mistakes that I am now the righteousness of God through Christ Jesus. When I am faithful to confess my sins, he is faithful to forgive (1 John 1:9, NIV).

So I confess and grow daily in the Spirit! But living for Satan is off the table. Living in sexual sin and helping bring others down with it is off the table. I am a new creation in Christ. All things are new, and the old me has passed away. I have peace and joy now through Jesus Christ, my high priest and intercessor! He is interceding for me now! I can't even imagine how I lived without submitting to God for so long. God kept his hand over me and protected me through so much. He wanted me to tell my story for his glory. My story shows what God can do to transform someone's life. There are so many powerful testimonies in others' lives that truly are amazing.

We have to tell people our testimonies and deny ourselves daily and follow after Christ Jesus. I do know that when you submit and follow him, all things are going to be new, clean, and pure. His grace and mercy make you want to become the better person he wants you to be through him! Accept his son Jesus today, quit fighting him, and just surrender! I promise you it will be the best decision of your life. Walk into his glory. I have peace now. The future does not scare me. The harvest is plentiful, but the workers are few! Let's work together and help spread the true gospel of Jesus Christ. Don't worry about family and friends who will mock you or leave you, for Jesus says no one is greater than their master. If they persecuted him, they will persecute us! I feel for all who are lost because some think they have found life in their spouse, car, house, or job. "For what does it profit a man to gain the whole world but lose his own soul?" (Mark 8:36, NIV).

The first few weeks after following Christ were purely amazing! I had never experienced such love, joy, and peace. I was like a ticking bomb ready to speak on the revelations the Holy Spirit was giving me. I felt so clean and pure as I was learning about my identity in Christ.

I will never forget the first time I met Jentezen Franklin. The Lord had been laying on my heart for me to meet him. At first, I was nervous. He was known worldwide! The Lord was asking me to share with him what had happened in my life and that God was calling me to speak out on the subject. I remember for a couple of weeks I would tell other people around the church and even other associate pastors about my testimony and that I felt led to speak up on this topic. The people I talked to at Free Chapel seemed to all direct me to someone else. Then I heard the Lord tell me, "I didn't ask you to tell them about your testimony and what I have called you to do. I told you to go to Jentezen." I was such a baby Christian. I know now God had so much patience with me, but he was right like he always is, and I had not listened.

The week before I was to talk to Jentezen, the Lord had me read the story of Esther. I thought, *Yes, she went straight to the king. She didn't try to do any side meetings with others.* Esther realized she could lose her life for speaking up, so I realized all I could lose was possibly some hurt feelings if there wasn't interest. That Sunday, I got in line to meet Jentezen after church and tell him my story. He was not what I was expecting at all. He was nice and friendly, and he took interest, especially when he saw the picture I showed him of me living as Scarlet. He asked for my name and my phone number, which I had already written down. He told me someone from church would be in contact and that he was happy and proud of me. I never heard anything that week from anyone from Free Chapel.

A few weeks later, I still hadn't heard anything. I get to Free Chapel early every Sunday so I can sit up front. I saw Jentezen that week talking to people after the first service right in front of where I sit, so I felt compelled to go and speak with him again. I wrote down my name and phone number again too. He said there was so much going on and that he would have someone from church contact me. I was excited again. He assured me it wasn't on purpose that I hadn't been contacted and someone would now contact me. That week I waited in eager expectation, but nobody contacted me. I waited a few more weeks, but no one called. I know now what was going on. The enemy was trying to discourage me and get me to walk in offense. The enemy came at me hard and said I wasn't anything to the body of Christ and that nobody cared about my story. He tried to make me feel offended and hurt by Jentezen and the church.

The Holy Spirit, my great comforter, comforted me during that time and showed me truth. He reminded me of Jentezen and how much he had touched my life during the darkest days of my transgender life. The Holy Spirit reminded me of how much he had revealed to me himself through Jentezen. I never once said anything bad about Jentezen or walked in offense from this situation like the old Jeffrey would have. I was saved. I couldn't even think bad thoughts about him because I really looked to him as a spiritual father. I followed the Holy Spirit, and the enemy was defeated by my obedience to God. I truly believe God was watching me at this time. He was watching to see if I would throw in the towel. God waited to see if I would be like Jacob or Esther, not giving up but contending for what I knew God was directing me to do.

The third time I went to Jentezen after a Sunday service, I could tell there was a difference. He apologized because they had just had conferences and there had been so much going on at Free Chapel. He took my name and number for the third time, and I saw him slip it in his coat pocket. I truly felt this time someone would contact me, and so it happened.

I was contacted that week by the young adult pastor there, and we planned a day to do dinner. I was so excited and ready to tell him of everything I was saved from and what God was laying on my heart to tell the world! He was supportive and very into hearing my testimony. That night at dinner, as I was saying it out loud to this pastor, I began to realize the magnitude of what God had called me to do. The enemy came in like a flood. *Are you really going to go into all the United States speaking on this homosexual/transgender* issue? *Are you really going to go to Thailand and help the "lady boys" there know Christ? This is huge, and you think God is going to uplift you to combat this stuff?* The enemy's lies were intimidating, but I knew God had called me for this and I would do these things. The young adult pastor was so encouraging and told me that night since God was calling me to do this, there was nothing that would hold it back. He told me finances, doors opening, and everything would come into place if God wanted me to do this. It was so encouraging!

One of the most awesome dreams I have had since I became a Christian involved Jentezen. I remember waking up one Sunday morning before church with a dream that just touched me so deeply. In the dream, I am sitting in a church meeting. My dad is sitting with me on my left. As I am sitting there, we are looking ahead on stage listening to Jentezen preach. Then I notice Jentezen is really sitting behind me, like the anointed Jentezen, and he reaches out his hand and touches my left shoulder while we are still looking at him speaking in front of us. When his hand is on my left shoulder, I can feel the anointing pouring out of him into my shoulder and body. Immediately in the dream, I tell God, "I want a double portion like Elisha" of the anointing that is flowing into me. I woke up and thought, *What an amazing dream!*

As I walked into Free Chapel that day, I saw Jentezen and others laying hands on people as they walked through a prayer chain. I remember thinking, *That is cool. I wonder what is going on.* We at Free Chapel had been on our annual twenty-one-day fast in January as a body together. I remember that was my first long fast, and in just the first few days, I had my prayer answered. I had wanted to share my testimony on television, and a television show had reached out to me about coming on to share my testimony. It was the last Sunday of the fast, and I was to find out that Sunday when Jentezen was anointing his hands and laying them on anyone as they walked through the prayer line. After the service, I of course decided to walk through the prayer line. When it was my turn, Jentezen laid his hand on my left shoulder in prayer! This was just a few hours after I'd had this dream. I remember also I had felt discouraged the past couple of weeks, and when Jentezen saw it was me, he patted my chest with this encouraging type of pat. It would seem so little to others, but that pat encouraged me for weeks. After that dream, and then literally hours later Jentezen actually laying his hands on me, I definitely never questioned God dreams again! God speaks through dreams a lot, so pay attention!

When I first applied to Christian television stations, I got a call back the next day. I was so ready to start sharing my testimony! A producer contacted me from one of the biggest Christian television stations. He asked me about my testimony and then asked how long I had been a Christian. When I told him I had been a Christian for only six months, he said, "Well, we like people like you to have come out of it for three years before we let them share." I was devastated. It was like the enemy had slammed me in the head with a two-by-four.

One night, shortly after I was woken up from sleep, I heard the word "Nightline." I knew it was from God, but I didn't really know what it meant. In the next couple of days, I remembered my dad had watched a program called *Nightline* from a local Christian television station. I looked up their info and sent my testimony to see about sharing on their show. Sure enough, just as God had planned, I received an email from the producer of the show asking me to be a guest and share my story! It was in January 2017 when she emailed me, but she wanted me to wait for a specific host who wanted to do my interview but wouldn't be hosting again until the end of March. I agreed and was looking forward to it! I know now I wasn't ready at the time, and the Lord was going to grow me during those three months to be prepared to share my testimony at the perfect time!

In January of 2017, a pastor from Tennessee reached out to me and asked me to share at her church. I was so excited! God had opened a door, and this time I hadn't had to beg to share my testimony—a pastor had asked me! She asked if I would share my story at a youth event at her church. I remember the night before the meeting, I was lying down on the couch at my mother's house. There above me hung a portrait of me and my brother Caleb. My father had given an artist photos of Caleb and me, and this artist had drawn us so well. I looked at that little boy. It was me before the hurt, sin, and shame that had enveloped my life. I was smiling and happy, not knowing what lay before me. I felt like that again because the Lord had restored me those previous months to knowing I am just his child and that he loves me. The Lord had cleansed me and was showing me my future. I was so excited for the next day to share my journey with others.

The next day came, and I started to get nervous. This was it! I had been begging God to be able to speak up and share what he had done in my life, and now the moment was set. The church was having a family-style supper, all eating together before the service started. I'll never forget asking the Holy Spirit to be with me and for me to feel some peace. When worship started, the peace came, and I could feel the presence of God there at that small community church. I was ready! I shared my testimony that night, and it was amazing. I shared on God's mercy and the love he had for me.

I got a call that day from another church asking me to speak the next morning at their Sunday service. I remember feeling so excited my first time to speak, and I got to share two days in a row! When I shared at the Sunday service the next day, I noticed someone I had grown up with. This guy was playing in the music band for worship that morning. This guy had never really liked me when we went to school together and was even mean to me on one occasion. I could see him looking at me almost like, *Why was I there at his church?* Then it was announced that I would be speaking. He never shook my hand after service or talked to me. The Lord was showing me that sometimes he has to humble some people so they can see his grace and mercy is for everyone, not just typical church people. He was showing them even ex-transsexuals can serve the Lord Jesus if they repent and turn to him. These were my first two experiences sharing my story in the body of Christ.

The next major ministry experience was the television show *Nightline*. The time passed, and before I knew it, the day was upon me. I remember the light and mirror in the dressing room. I remember at that moment feeling a little nervous and thinking of my old best friend who used to help me get dressed and ready before my drag shows. I missed him and felt somewhat alone, but I prayed and knew my Father in heaven was with me. I didn't need a dresser or helper for this; I just needed the Holy Spirit. I think of that friend sometimes when getting ready for television shows.

I felt so calm right before. When the other guests arrived, they asked if I was nervous, but I said no. I really wasn't. The Holy Spirit was with me, and God had given me the grace to do this assignment.

The host, Keith Kelley, did a wonderful job! The show runs about an hour and half, and before the show, the producer told me I would be on the bulk of the show—almost the whole first hour. The Holy Spirit took over and got me to cover exactly what he wanted to say. I'll never forget, before I left, a woman called in and told me how well I had done and that she was encouraged by my testimony! It meant so much to hear those words. Days later, I got an email from a parent who had a child who was going through some of the same stuff I had. It was powerful to see I had helped encourage the body of Christ that had family involved in this sin. I learned early on God was wanting me to speak at churches and Christian venues because he wanted to go to his body first and let them know there is hope for their loved ones also.

Two days after the television show, I experienced spiritual warfare like never before. I remember that night feeling darkness around me that I had not felt as a Christian. I felt torment and fear coming toward me. It was the first time I experienced the spirit of intimidation, and it was strong. I realize now looking back how the principalities involved with homosexuality were angry with what I had done. God grew me during this time because God knew the big journey I had ahead, and he was watching to see what I would do. I remember one night feeling so far from God, as if he had left me. I had to learn early on I couldn't go off of my feelings like I had done in the world. The righteous live by faith. God grew my faith in him so much during this time of battle with the spirit of intimidation. I remember one night just saying, "Lord, if you have left me, I will still direct people to you, I will still say you are God,

I will still say Jesus is Lord." I didn't know what else to do. I had to have faith that he was with me even though I felt like he was gone. He was with me the whole time this lasted, about six weeks. It eventually broke, and I could feel his presence again.

After becoming a Christian, I got close to a woman named Kasondra Watkins. I had grown up with Kasondra in a small county in Tennessee, and we had gone to school together for a few years. She had overcome so many odds and become a Christian also. The Lord knew I needed her, because during this time, he was revealing so much of himself to me, and I needed another Christian to discuss these things with. She saw the calling on my life and fed into what Jesus was doing through me. I was actually talking to her the second time I got a strong prophetic word that would guide me into my work for Christ. I was on the phone with her while she was in New York City. She was staying with a man named T. Kasondra and I were FaceTiming, and she handed the phone to him. After about two minutes on the phone, he started prophesying to me. He told me the Lord had great plans for me and the Lord was going to take me all over the US. He also said he saw a CD teaching and a book in my future! He told me the Lord loved me very much, and he had trusted me with this platform. He also told me there would be healings brought forth because of my compassion for people! I also learned God wanted me to have my own children and that I would be married one day! He said God said I would make a great father, and he wanted children to experience how great of a father I would be. I also learned shame and guilt would break off of people with my ministry! I was shocked! The Lord had been showing me some of these plans, but to come from someone who didn't know what those were was amazing! It was a word that highly propelled me to move forward and continue in excitement with what the Lord was going to use me to do.

I highly suggest if you are hungry for more of the Lord to surround yourself with people who walk in the gifts of the Holy Spirit, because these gifts help launch, edify, and encourage us Christians. God said in his word, "Where there is no vision, the people tarry," and I learned early on to hold tight to prophetic words. This is why Paul instructs Timothy to hold on to the prophetic word he was given. Real prophets don't always tell you what you want to hear; they tell you what God is saying to you. This was one word, though, that propelled me and kept me encouraged. To think God trusted me with this assignment really helped me see myself as his son!

May of 2017 was my thirtieth birthday. Things shifted heavily in this month, and the work was on overload. I had an interview for the Fringe Network with a guy from Taiwan. The same day, I had a radio interview with a lady traveling the country to promote truth. I was invited to record my testimony at another Christian television program in Atlanta, Georgia. Then I was invited to record my testimony in two interviews in Alabama. Another church opened up in Tennessee for me to speak at. The work was definitely picking up. The trip from Alabama to Tennessee where I was going to speak was an interesting one.

After I was done filming the interviews in Alabama, I felt the Holy Spirit drawing me to Tennessee. I didn't necessarily want to go there. I wanted to go back home to Georgia to my bed and rest after a long weekend in Alabama at a friend's home. I followed the Holy Spirit's tugging and decided I would go to Tennessee and see my family there, even though I was about to go on vacation with them a week later. I had no clue why the Holy Spirit was calling me to Tennessee.

I typed in my mother's address in my GPS and followed the route from Gadsden, Alabama, to Shelbyville, Tennessee. I put on some worship music and was intently into it. As I was driving and worshipping, I saw a town sign saying, "Welcome to Guntersville, Alabama." Guntersville was where my paternal grandmother's family was from and had lived for a couple of generations. I had been watching a lot of Sid Roth the previous month and learning from older Christians about breaking bloodline curses, and also about calling in blessings from your ancestors after the curses were broken. I felt the Holy Spirit showing me that he had brought me along this specific route to go exactly through my ancestors' town!

I felt led to pull over and touch my feet to that ground and call back all the blessings from that bloodline. I got out at a stop where there is a clearing by the beautiful river that runs through that town. There were men fishing there, but I didn't care. I started praying, not too loud, so I wouldn't scare them, and calling back all bloodline blessings! I got back in the car and started playing my worship music again. As I was enjoying my worship, I thought, *How amazing was that opportunity God had just given me?*

The next stop I would be coming to was Huntsville, Alabama. This was the city I was born in! I thought, *How interesting—God brings me to film my testimony in my home state where I was born, and then to go through Guntersville where some of my ancestors were from, and now going to the actual city where I was born.* As I was coming into Huntsville on this road I have never been on, I heard the Holy Spirit say to me, "Go to Huntsville Hospital where you were born."

I said, "God, I can't do that right now. I'll have to change the GPS address, and I'll have to change route, and I don't know exactly where I am at." I was literally talking back to God!

As I looked up at the red light right in front of me where I was arguing with God, I saw the big sign: Huntsville Hospital. The hospital was right in front of me the whole time! In this large city, I had been perfectly brought in by a side road to be strategically where God wanted me to go! If I would have said yes, it was right there in front of me, it would have been an even bigger blessing because I would have walked in obedience and then seen where I was. I was in shock somewhat because there it was right in front of me! I asked God to forgive me and felt horrible for one second, then pulled in. I knew God forgave me and was just showing me once again to listen to him and walk in obedience. Then God told me of all the places in this world, this was the spot he chose to birth the seed of Jeffrey Abraham McCall. He told me to claim back my blessings, my destiny, and the things the enemy tried to steal from me right there from the beginning. I got out, put my feet on the grass, and prayed and claimed back all of it, including my destiny! I got back in the car and drove toward Tennessee. I was thinking, *What an amazing trip!* Then I hit the Tennessee state line.

When I entered Tennessee, I could see clouds and darkness on my left toward Shelbyville, the town where I was heading. This was the town I had grown up in and where my mother still lives. I could feel darkness and see it manifesting in the storms, and it felt different. I knew I was supposed to release a word and speak there. I contacted a pastor I knew who had been my youth pastor when I was younger. He let me release my testimony at his church and even pray for people afterward. It was the first time at a church sharing that I didn't feel nervous at all, but just went straight into it! It was amazing, and I want to encourage people to listen to the Holy Spirit and release where he gives you authority and where he sends you to release. We don't want to be like Jonah and go through horrible experiences because we will not release God's word in a place at his timing.

Before sharing that night, I remember going to my maternal grandmother's nursing home. I always called her my "Mima," and I had wanted to see her and felt drawn to go to her. When I did, it was amazing! I brought her favorite sandwich, and we ate together. She has been a Spirit-filled Christian my whole life and is the one who prophesied over me when I was born. Little did I know that she was going to impart in me that day spiritual blessings.

I remember after dinner I was talking to her about the work I was doing for the Lord and the excitement I had for the Holy Spirit and the healings and miracles that had occurred through other ministries. She told me about her experience going to see Kathryn Kuhlman and other evangelists. She started praying for me and told me from the moment I had left my old life and followed Jesus, God had been with me. She prayed a blessing over me and prayed that I would preach the gospel. She then told me to get her anointing oil. She told me she doesn't play with her anointed oil and that's why she had it hidden in a purse in the closet. I went into the closet and brought her the oil. She anointed me and then asked me to open my hands. She anointed them with oil too, and I remember feeling fire in my body, but specifically in my hands! It was an amazing experience, and the Lord encouraged me much through my grandmother that day.

One experience I had occurred that same summer. I was watching Michael Koulianos, Benny Hinn's son-in-law, preaching a sermon. I started feeling a strong feeling come over my body. For three days, it felt like electricity was running through my body. I felt like I was being spiritually deep-cleaned. I had to read my Bible every thirty minutes! I felt so alive, clean, and pure! I will never forget that experience. My addiction to pornography was broken during those days. I fell afterward at times with looking at pornography, but the addiction of it was broken during that time. When the power of the Holy Spirit comes upon you, situations you have been struggling to deal with on your own for years can be lifted in seconds!

The supernatural just kept occurring, and I experienced God daily in different ways! A lot had been happening recently at night and in my dreams. In one dream, I could see inside my knee! It had crystal-clear glass over the kneecap, and I could see this beautiful, thick, golden honey. A heavenly person was standing beside me and telling me to look inside. I was so excited seeing the heavenly honey inside me! Where the bones would meet in the knee was a honeycomb with four bees working in it. I later got the interpretation from a fellow brother that the honey was what the Lord had been building in me and that he was now letting me see the manifestation of the work he had been doing in me. The four bees represented people he was using to grow in me four different gifts God had given me! It was soon after this dream I finally saw the first healing of someone I had prayed for.

Since this dream, I have seen the Lord manifest so much of his power in my life. Another supernatural event occurred when I woke up and didn't know where I was but could see in the Spirit my right hand wrapped in white linen. It was absolutely amazing! I have hints of what it means, but I don't have the full revelation yet. Also, there was one night when I woke up and felt the kingdom of heaven was in my room, like it was glory from the realm of heaven! It's amazing how exciting every day is when you accept Jesus Christ and turn from sin and live for him. He has made life fuller and more exciting than any sin can be. When the enemy reminds me of temporary pleasures of sin, I can feel the Holy Spirit showing me the amazing, peace-filled life I have now through Jesus Christ. Jesus said he would give us life and more abundant life. When we walk in the Spirit and not in the flesh, life is must indescribably victorious, amazing, and vibrant!

I also started getting words of knowledge around 2017. I had to take a drug test for the professor job I had accepted. I thanked the nurse who helped me and then turned to leave. I heard the Holy Spirit say the word "father," and I immediately knew it was about the nurse's dad. I didn't stop and pray with her then but walked to my car. I sat down and spoke out loud to God. I asked God, "If this is you, definitely confirm it is and tell me now if you want me to go back in and talk to her about her dad." The enemy had come to me with doubt and unbelief when the Holy Spirit had pressed the word "father" on my spirit.

But I heard the Holy Spirit say, "If you don't go back in and tell her what I showed you, it will be three months before you get a word for someone else. Think of all the people you can minister to in three months!"

I obeyed and walked back in. I asked the lady if she had a father who was living. She told me yes and looked stunned. I asked if there was something going on with him, and she teared up. I told her God had told me the word "father" for her and wanted me to pray with her, but I had left and gone out to car. I told her I had prayed and that I had to come back in. She was amazed and told me the hairs were standing up on her arm. She was stunned and kept saying this whole thing was from God and such a testimony to her. It turned out her father had colon cancer twenty years ago and it had recently come back. He was going through chemo treatments and having a hard time. She was so thankful I had come back. She got to see God thinking of her through me being obedient and showing her through a word that God was thinking of her and her father's situation! I love the gift of words of knowledge. In an instant, you know something no one else would know except God, and it shows people God is thinking of them and their value to him.

From the beginning of my Christian walk, I have believed the God of Abraham, Isaac, and Jacob still heals today. Jesus would not have said we would lay our hands on the sick and they would recover if he didn't want us to do it. When the words of knowledge started, a lot of them were for people's physical healing. I would get direct words for people about physical ailments and would step out in faith and pray for them.

One story involves an African American man I saw walking out of the grocery store. When I saw him, I knew he needed prayer for his right knee and even knew specifically it was pain behind his right knee in the back of the leg. I walked up to him in faith and asked him about his knee and told him I even knew exactly where the pain was. He looked at me in shock and told me there was pain in that exact spot. I reached down and put my hands on the spot and prayed for him. He thanked me and got in his car and left.

I got so many of these words for people but never saw the physical manifestation of healing in those moments. God was watching me and seeing my obedience and seeing if I was going to keep going and praying for people even if it didn't seem anything was happening. Faith won, and I continued to step out and pray for people even if I didn't see anything. In 2018, I began to see the physical manifestations of people healed. I still remember the first few times—it even shocked me!

I believe God can use any of his children who follow Jesus Christ if we will just step out in faith. He is a supernatural God! I want to encourage everyone reading this, if you are a Christian, keep stepping out in faith that he will use you. The enemy will come to lie, and so many Christian denominations share that healing is not for today, when Jesus commanded us to pray for the sick.

One day, I encountered the spirit that tries to bring in these lies. I was lying on my bed and thinking of some of the healings I had seen the Lord work. All of a sudden, I felt the presence of something heavy. I heard in my mind that "healing is not for today, God did those things before but not really for now."

Then I heard the Holy Spirit's voice on my right side. The Holy Spirit said, "Open the book of Mark and read the ending."

I read where Jesus says, "And these signs will accompany those who believe: In my name they will drive out demons; they will speak in new tongues, they will pick up snakes with their hands; and when they drink deadly poison; it will not hurt them at all; they will place their hands on sick people and they will get well" (Mark 16:17–18, NIV).

After I read it out loud, the Holy Spirit directed me to

read it two more times. After the third time, the demonic spirit left. The Lord showed me how much we have to be in tune with the Holy Spirit and be open to his guidance and direction. Without the Holy Spirit, I would have been deceived that day, like so many have been in the body of Christ. Healing is for today, and I will never give in to those spirits that want us to believe God is not a supernatural, miraculous God!

If God didn't want to use us Christians to pray and manifest healings on others, why would he say we would do it? He is not a liar, but everything in this world hangs on his words. Colossians tells us everything in this world was created by Jesus and for Jesus. The book of John tells us Jesus is the word made manifest! If the word of God, Jesus, tells us to do something, then it is possible. We must believe him over any denominational teaching!

So why would I write my story and tell of all the things I went through and the embarrassing details of shame in my own life? I do this to give everyone the hope of Jesus Christ. He is the only way, and he can save you also! The supernatural experiences are awesome, and I love seeing how God works, but it's Jesus sacrifice and his love for me that are most important. To think the word became flesh and died for you and me is absolutely heartbreaking, yet the most special love ever!

Let that soak in. Think of how much you are actually worth. You are worth more than gold, rubies, or diamonds. The highest cost had to be paid for you. Jesus, the son of God, was payment for you. He didn't have to leave heaven to become flesh and live in this fallen world and become sin, but he did because he loves us so much and thinks so highly of us that he wanted us to be sons and daughters of God also! The Father loves us so much. Every hurt and every pain you have gone through is something I believe the enemy will use to try to separate you from your faith in God.

The Holy Spirit right now is even showing me people reading this who are feeling conviction of their sin and separation from God. All you have to do is put your faith in Jesus Christ. Believe he died for your sins and was raised by God from the dead, and you shall be saved! "That if you confess with your mouth the Lord Jesus and believe in your heart that God has raised him from the dead, you will be saved" (Romans 10:9, NIV).

If you just put your faith in Jesus Christ, then ask the Holy Spirit to fill you! The Holy Spirit is your great teacher and comforter now. Jesus sent him to you! I truly believe Jesus sent us believers the Holy Spirit, because he tells us that in his word. I am so excited for your journey because Jesus has set you, another captive, free from sin. Get ready to start a relationship with the creator of the universe, but also the creator of you!

About the Author

Jeffrey McCall runs a ministry called For Such a Time. He resides in Franklin Springs, Georgia. Jeffrey travels the country sharing his testimony at churches, on television, on radio, and at public events. He is the visionary founder and CEO of Freedom Marches. The Freedom Marches are events where people who left LGBTQ lifestyles share their stories and march together for freedom through Jesus Christ. Jeffrey has a bachelor's degree in history from Emmanuel College and a master's degree in history from East Tennessee State University.